TWISTED JOURNEYS® #5

NIGHTMARE ON ZOMBIE ISLAND

PAUL D STORRIE

ILLUSTRATED BY DAVID WITT

Lerner

Story by Paul D Storrie

Pencils and inks by David Witt

Colouring by Hi-Fi Design

Lettering by Marshall Dillon and Terri Delgado

Graphic Universe™ is a trademark and Twisted Journeys® is a registered trademark
of Lerner Publishing Group, Inc.

First published in the United Kingdom in 2009 by
Lerner Books,
Dalton House,
60 Windsor Avenue,
London SW19 2RR

Website address: www.lernerbooks.co.uk

This edition was updated and edited for UK publication by Discovery Books Ltd.,
First Floor, 2 College Street, Ludlow, Shropshire SY8 1AN

British Library Cataloguing in Publication Data

Storrie, Paul D
  Nightmare on Zombie Island. - 2nd ed. - (Twisted journeys)
  1. Plot-your-own stories 2. Children's stories - Comic
  books, strips, etc.
  I. Title
  741.5

ISBN-13: 978 0 7613 4410 0

ARE YOU READY FOR YOUR **Twisted Journeys®?** *YOU* ARE THE HERO OF THE BOOK YOU'RE ABOUT TO READ. YOUR JOURNEYS WILL BE PACKED WITH ADVENTURES AS YOU JOIN A TEAM OF EXPLORERS ON A LEGENDARY ISLAND. AND EVERY STORY STARS *YOU!*

EACH PAGE TELLS WHAT HAPPENS TO *YOU* AS YOU TRY TO ESCAPE THE ZOMBIE CURSE. *YOUR* WORDS AND THOUGHTS ARE SHOWN IN THE *YELLOW BALLOONS.* AND YOU GET TO DECIDE WHAT HAPPENS NEXT. JUST FOLLOW THE NOTE AT THE BOTTOM OF EACH PAGE UNTIL YOU REACH A **Twisted Journeys®** PAGE. THEN MAKE THE CHOICE *YOU* LIKE BEST.

BUT BE CAREFUL . . . THE WRONG CHOICE COULD MAKE YOUR HOLIDAY ON ZOMBIE ISLAND VERY SHORT!

You still can't believe your parents are letting you spend the summer with your best friend Jimmy and his aunt, Dr Elizabeth Chase. She is a world-famous explorer. Dr Chase and her assistants are here to discover why the plantation on this island was abandoned two hundred years ago. Sure, you have to help out a little, but mostly you plan to have fun!

You arrive on the *Marlin*, a charter boat owned by Captain Skip Allen. Since there's no dock on the island, he uses an inflatable motor-boat to bring everyone ashore.

As you get ready to hike to the campsite by the plantation house, Jimmy says, 'This is going to be great!' You can't help grinning.

'This is a *terrible* place,' says someone behind you.

You both jump in surprise. It's Dylan, the *Marlin*'s only crewman.

You ask what he means.

Dylan leans closer and says softly, 'It's like this . . . '

BLOODY BOB SLADE WAS THE NASTIEST PIRATE IN ALL THE CARIBBEAN.

LEGEND TELLS THAT HE HID HIS TREASURE IN A CAVE ON THIS ISLAND TO KEEP IT SAFE. ONLY SOMETHING HAPPENED THAT HE NEVER EXPECTED ...

WHILE HE WAS AWAY PIRATING, SOMEONE SET UP A PLANTATION ON THE ISLAND. WHEN HE RETURNED AND FOUND OUT, HE WAS FURIOUS.

AFRAID THAT THE PIRATES WOULD ONE DAY KILL THEM TOO, THEY ASKED THEIR WISE WOMAN WHAT TO DO.

HE KILLED THE PLANTATION OWNERS BUT KEPT THEIR SERVANTS ALIVE TO WAIT ON HIM AND HIS CREW.

GO ON TO THE NEXT PAGE.

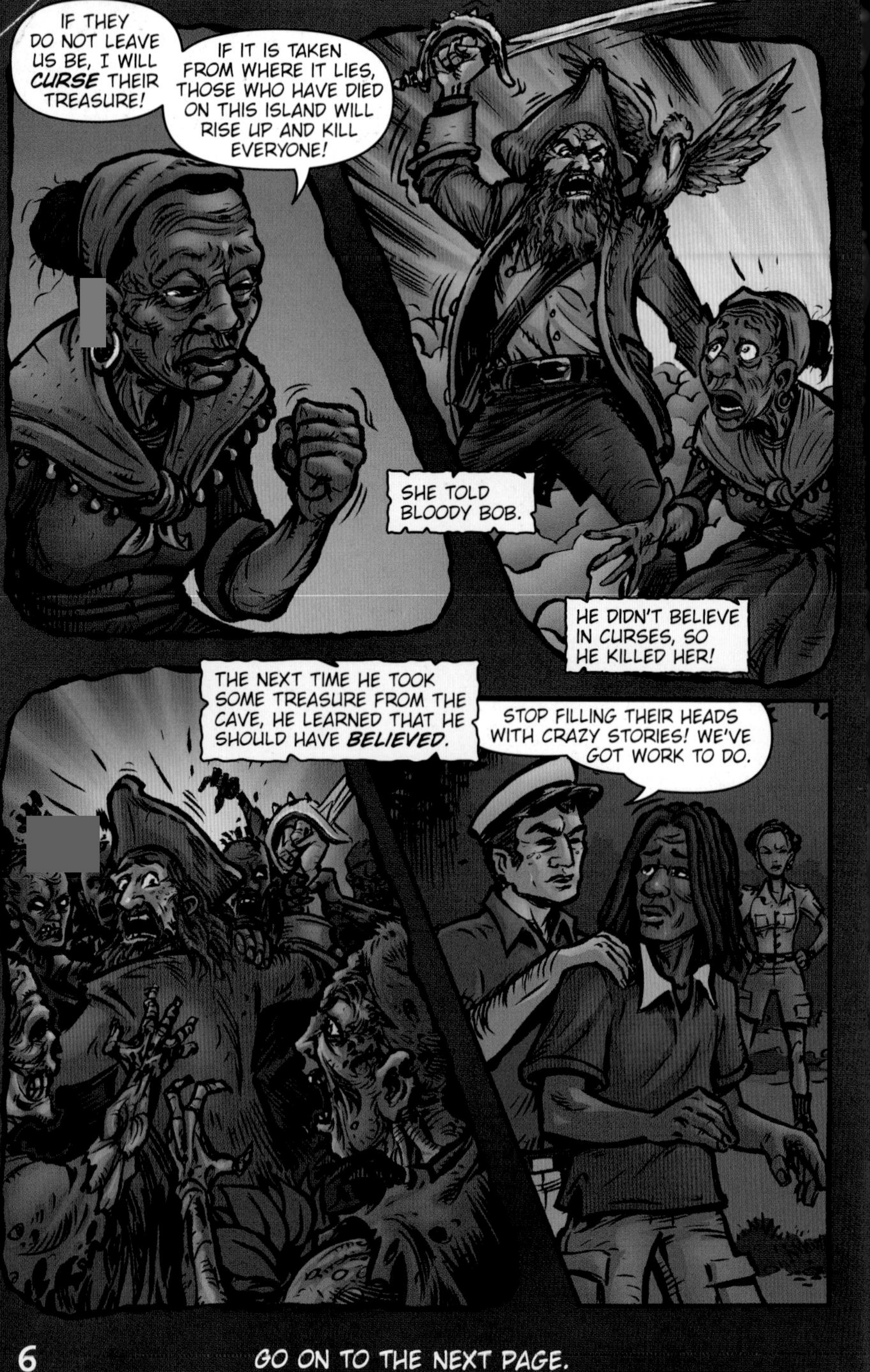
IF THEY DO NOT LEAVE US BE, I WILL CURSE THEIR TREASURE!
IF IT IS TAKEN FROM WHERE IT LIES, THOSE WHO HAVE DIED ON THIS ISLAND WILL RISE UP AND KILL EVERYONE!
SHE TOLD BLOODY BOB.
HE DIDN'T BELIEVE IN CURSES, SO HE KILLED HER!
THE NEXT TIME HE TOOK SOME TREASURE FROM THE CAVE, HE LEARNED THAT HE SHOULD HAVE BELIEVED.
STOP FILLING THEIR HEADS WITH CRAZY STORIES! WE'VE GOT WORK TO DO.

GO ON TO THE NEXT PAGE.

Dr Chase comes over and says you and Jimmy ca[n]
stay on the beach and play if you want. Otherwise,
you have to help set up camp. Jimmy says he wants
to stay, but you wonder if Dylan has more to tell you.

WILL YOU ...

... stay on the beach?
TURN TO PAGE 18.

... help set up camp and
maybe hear more of Dylan's story?
TURN TO PAGE 22.

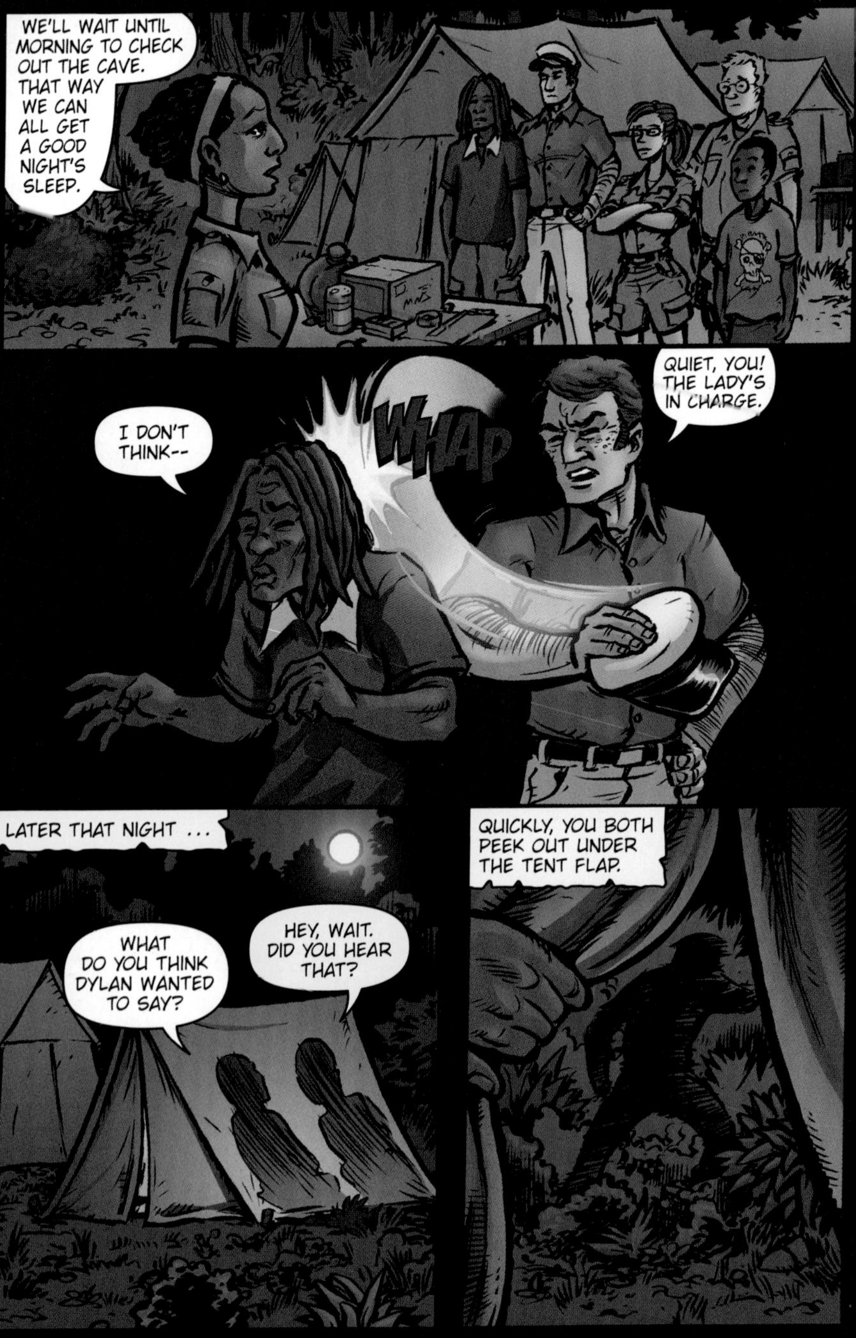
WE'LL WAIT UNTIL MORNING TO CHECK OUT THE CAVE. THAT WAY WE CAN ALL GET A GOOD NIGHT'S SLEEP.
I DON'T THINK--
WHAP
QUIET, YOU! THE LADY'S IN CHARGE.
LATER THAT NIGHT . . .
WHAT DO YOU THINK DYLAN WANTED TO SAY?
HEY, WAIT. DID YOU HEAR THAT?
QUICKLY, YOU BOTH PEEK OUT UNDER THE TENT FLAP.

TURN TO PAGE 97.

'He was the one who wanted to go back to the *Marlin*,' you say.

Partway back to the camp, the captain says he needs to rest. He puts his back to a tree and gradually eases himself to the ground, careful not to spill any treasure.

'Fine,' grumbles Dr Chase. She sits down herself and starts poking around in the box she's carrying.

A minute or two later, you hear someone coming through the trees.

'Syd?' Dr Chase calls out. 'Marty?'

Then a crowd of strangers staggers out of the shadows. Moonlight shines on their blank eyes and slack-jawed faces.

'Zombies!' you scream.

The captain jumps to his feet, spilling coins and jewels everywhere.

You try to run, but you slip on some of the fallen gems and crash into the ground.

The last thing you see is a pair of bare feet with nasty, cracked toenails in the dirt in front of you.

THE END

'We should keep going,' you say. 'Dylan seemed pretty desperate.'

Syd puts a sympathetic hand on her brother's shoulder. 'Why don't you kids go on down to the lagoon?' she says. 'I'll wait here with Marty. We'll be there soon.'

You pull Jimmy along with you and call back, 'See you soon!'

You're just glad to be moving again.

When you get to the lagoon, you find Dylan and the captain arguing about what to do. Dylan is in the motorboat and wants to start the engine.

'Where are the others?' he asks. 'We should get out to the *Marlin*.'

'They'll be here in a minute,' says Jimmy.

Suddenly, loud scream- ing splits the quiet night.

'Is that Syd and Marty?' Jimmy gasps. 'Should we go back?'

'It's too late!' Dylan yells, pointing towards the trees. 'Look!'

THE CAPTAIN JUST ABOUT THROWS YOU AND JIMMY INTO THE MOTORBOAT AS DYLAN STARTS THE ENGINE. YOU CAN'T BELIEVE WHAT YOU'RE SEEING!

ARRRRH!!

UHHHNG!

EVEN WHEN THE MOTORBOAT PULLS AWAY FROM THE SHORE, THEY KEEP COMING!

AS YOU CLIMB ONTO THE *MARLIN*, YOU SHOUT TO DYLAN THAT THEY'RE STILL COMING!

I THINK WE'LL BE OKAY ONCE WE'RE IN OPEN WATER!

YOU HOPE HE'S RIGHT. MAYBE YOU REALLY HAVE *ESCAPED* FROM *ZOMBIE ISLAND!*

THE END

11

'Maybe there *is* some kind of curse,' you say. 'Why hasn't anybody lived here for so long?'

'That's a good point!' Jimmy agrees. 'What if there is a curse?'

Dr Chase gives Dylan a dirty look, but then she smiles and says, 'If it'll make you children feel any better, we won't bother with the caves this trip.'

'But, Dr Chase,' says Syd, 'Bloody Bob's treasure would be a tremendous historical find!'

'Yes, it would,' says Dr Chase. 'But if it's there, it's not going anywhere. It can wait.'

With that, she takes Syd and Marty into the plantation house to look around.

You and Jimmy decide to play hide-and-seek around the campsite. An hour or so later, while you're hiding from Jimmy, you see Dr Chase sneak out of the house.

She looks around but doesn't see you.

Then she heads off towards the waterfall.

GO ON TO THE NEXT PAGE.

WILL YOU . . .

. . . go up to the plantation and tell the others?
TURN TO PAGE 16.

. . . get Jimmy and follow his aunt?
TURN TO PAGE 25.

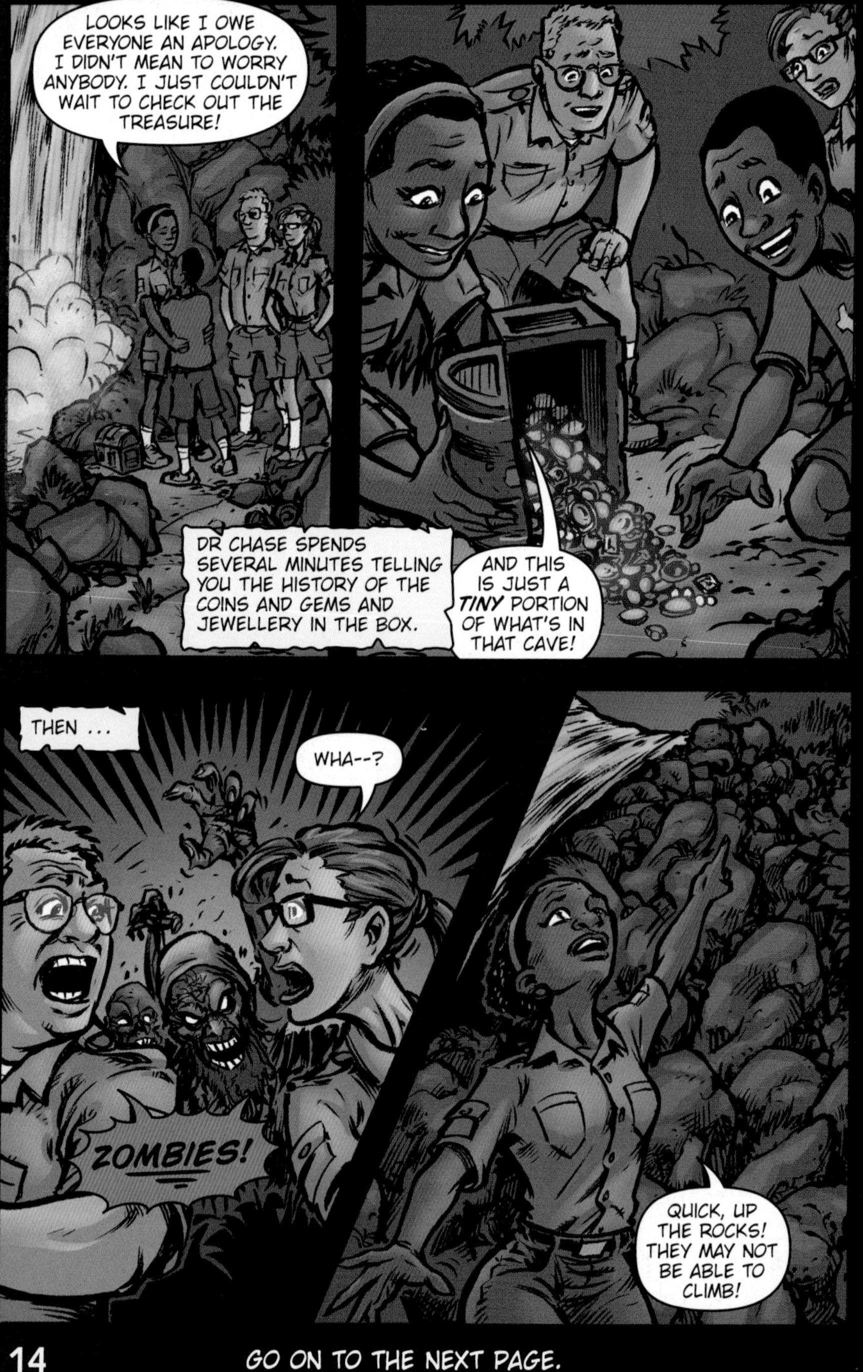
LOOKS LIKE I OWE EVERYONE AN APOLOGY. I DIDN'T MEAN TO WORRY ANYBODY. I JUST COULDN'T WAIT TO CHECK OUT THE TREASURE!
DR CHASE SPENDS SEVERAL MINUTES TELLING YOU THE HISTORY OF THE COINS AND GEMS AND JEWELLERY IN THE BOX.
AND THIS IS JUST A *TINY* PORTION OF WHAT'S IN THAT CAVE!
THEN ...
WHA--?
ZOMBIES!
QUICK, UP THE ROCKS! THEY MAY NOT BE ABLE TO CLIMB!

GO ON TO THE NEXT PAGE.

The five of you manage to scramble up the short cliff. One of the zombies grabs Marty by the leg halfway up, but Syd manages to pull him away.

Then the zombies slowly begin to climb themselves!

'I hear waves!' yells Jimmy.

Thinking you might be able to swim to the *Marlin*, you all scramble over the rocky ground towards the sound of the sea. The crashing of waves gets louder.

'We're almost there!' you cry.

Rushing up the last hill, your spirits soar. Then they crash down.

There's a 10-metre drop to the water and jagged rocks below.

'We've got to turn back,' you say. 'Try another way.'

Then a small shape drops out of the darkness, clawing at your face. It's Bloody Bob's parrot! A zombie parrot!

Stumbling back, you tumble over the cliff and drop towards the crashing waves below.

THE END

You rush up to the house and yell for Syd and Marty. By the time they come out, Jimmy, the captain, and Dylan have shown up too.

'Why all the yelling?' asks the captain.

You explain about Dr Chase slipping off towards the treasure after she said she wouldn't.

'This isn't good!' exclaims Dylan. 'She's going to bring that curse down on us all!'

'Don't be silly,' says Syd. 'She probably just wanted to check out the treasure without you getting the children all panicked about your stupid curse!'

'I'm going to the *Marlin*!' shouts Dylan, heading for the lagoon. 'If you're smart, you'll all come too!'

The captain throws his hands up in the air and says, 'I'd better go and make sure he doesn't leave us stranded here.'

'I'm going to find my aunt!' says Jimmy. Then he takes off towards the waterfall.

'I guess we should go after him,' Marty moans.

GO ON TO THE NEXT PAGE.

WILL YOU . . .

. . . follow Jimmy?
TURN TO PAGE 14.

. . . follow Dylan to the *Marlin*?
TURN TO PAGE 28.

A couple of minutes after everyone else has left the beach, Jimmy picks up his backpack.

'Let's explore the island!' he says. Without waiting for you to answer, he marches off under the trees.

Grabbing your bag, you rush after him.

There's a stream feeding into the lagoon, and Jimmy says you should follow it. The stream winds through the trees, until it ends in a clearing. There's a small pool there fed by a waterfall that splashes off a short cliff.

'Hey, why don't we make this our 'base camp'?' you suggest. 'Leave our stuff and explore out from here.'

Jimmy agrees, and you spend hours hiking and climbing rocks. Eventually, you end up back at the pool and start skimming stones.

You toss one that skims four times before it splashes into the waterfall. After a second, you hear the clatter of stone on stone.

'That's weird,' says Jimmy.

GO ON TO THE NEXT PAGE.

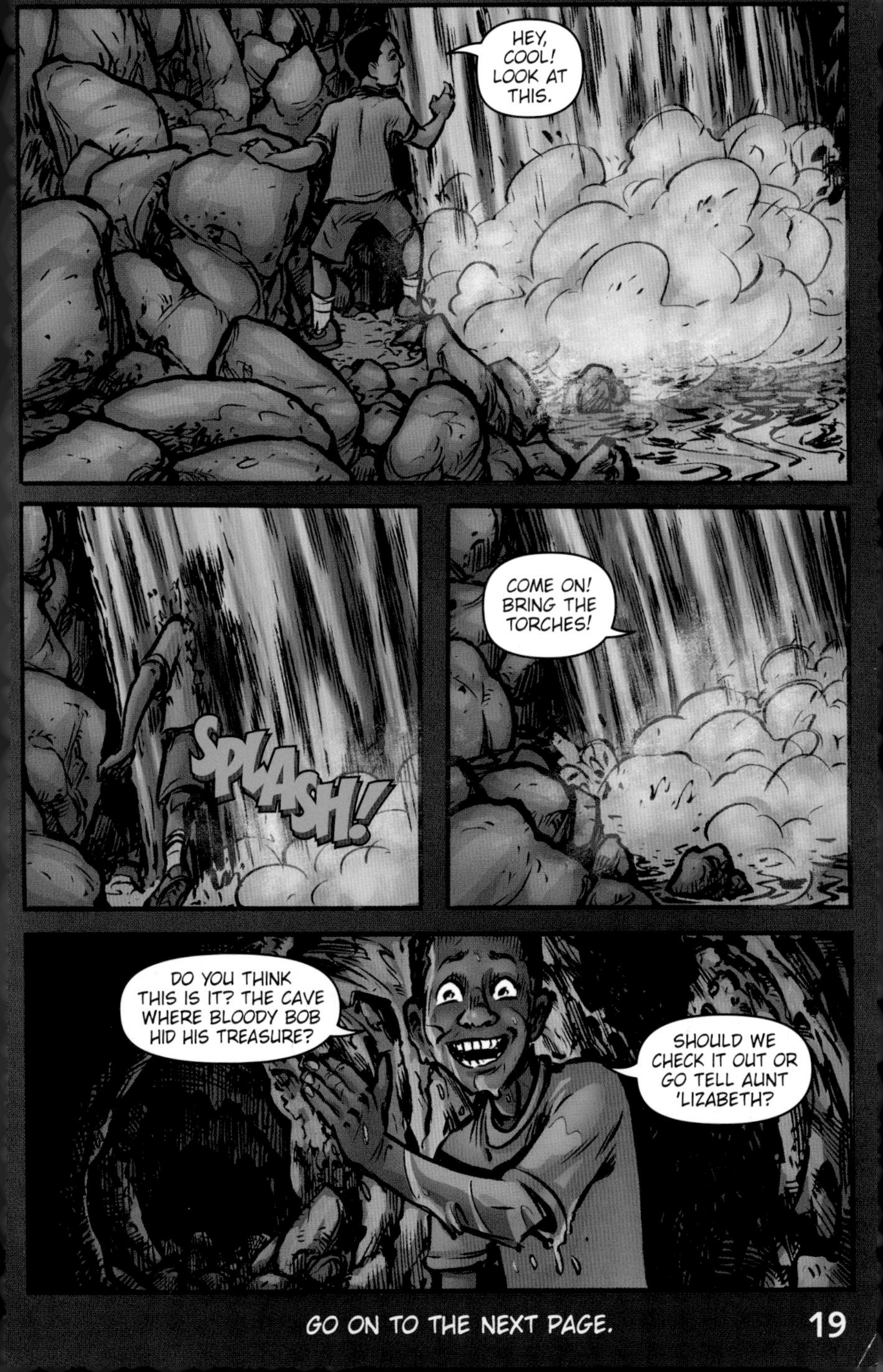
HEY, COOL! LOOK AT THIS.
SPLASH!
COME ON! BRING THE TORCHES!
DO YOU THINK THIS IS IT? THE CAVE WHERE BLOODY BOB HID HIS TREASURE?
SHOULD WE CHECK IT OUT OR GO TELL AUNT 'LIZABETH?

GO ON TO THE NEXT PAGE.

WILL YOU . . .

... and Jimmy go and explore the cave?

TURN TO PAGE 43.

... go to the camp and tell Dr Chase?

TURN TO PAGE 54.

'The motor will be faster!' you yell. Everybody seems to agree.

Dr Chase cranks the engine again and again. Then Dylan tells her to let him try. She starts to argue, but is cut off as Jimmy cries out, 'They're here!'

Dylan and Dr Chase fumble for the oars. You and Jimmy yell at them to go quicker.

Too late! The zombies grab the motorboat and haul themselves in. Dylan tries to smack them with the paddle, but it works no better than the stick Syd tried earlier.

The motorboat lurches as the zombies pull one end under the water. You tumble backwards, hitting the cold seawater.

Then you feel even colder hands on your legs, pulling you under . . .

THE END

YOU FOLLOW AN OVERGROWN TRAIL TO THE PLANTATION HOUSE. DR CHASE WANTS TO CAMP CLOSE BY, SINCE SHE AND HER ASSISTANTS ARE HERE TO STUDY IT.

SYD, WHY DON'T YOU GET STARTED ON YOUR TENT? MARTY CAN HELP ME HERE.

ALRIGHT, DR CHASE.

AFTER YOUR TENT IS UP, YOU ASK DYLAN TO TELL YOU MORE ABOUT THE CURSE.

ONLY TWO THINGS WILL STOP ZOMBIES. YOU CAN TRY CUTTING THEM UP IN LITTLE PIECES.

BUT THE BEST WAY IS TO THROW *SALT* IN THEIR MOUTHS.

THEY SAY IT REMINDS THE WALKING DEAD OF THE LIFE THAT THEY'VE LOST AND SENDS THEM BACK TO THEIR GRAVES!

SALT

GO ON TO THE NEXT PAGE.

Making sure no one sees, he gives you and Jimmy each a pot of salt and says, 'Keep it with you.'

That night, as you and Jimmy sit up talking by the light of your torches, you ask Jimmy if he thinks Dylan was serious.

'I don't know,' Jimmy says. 'He seemed serious. But zombies? They're only in films.'

A noise outside catches your attention. You and Jimmy turn off your torches, then peer out from under the front flap of your tent.

There's just enough moonlight to make out a shadowy figure leaving the camp and vanishing into the darkness under the trees!

'That's strange,' says Jimmy. 'What should we do?'

GO ON TO THE NEXT PAGE.

WILL YOU . . .

. . . wake up Dr Chase and let her know?
TURN TO PAGE 30.

. . . and Jimmy follow the shadowy figure on your own?
TURN TO PAGE 60.

When you find Jimmy, he starts to joke about how you don't know how to play hide-and-seek.

'Forget that!' you say. 'I just saw your aunt sneak off towards the cave!'

Jimmy looks puzzled. 'Why would she do that? She said she was going to leave it alone.'

'I don't know!' you exclaim. 'Let's go find out what she's doing.'

It takes a few minutes to convince Jimmy, but finally he agrees. The two of you hurry though the trees towards the waterfall.

When you get to the clearing, there's no sign of Dr Chase.

'She must have gone in,' you say. 'Let's follow her!'

'I don't know,' Jimmy says. 'She might get angry.'

While you're arguing, you hear a loud splashing. Turning, you see Dr Chase standing near the waterfall staring at you in surprise. She's holding a small wooden chest under one arm.

GO ON TO THE NEXT PAGE.

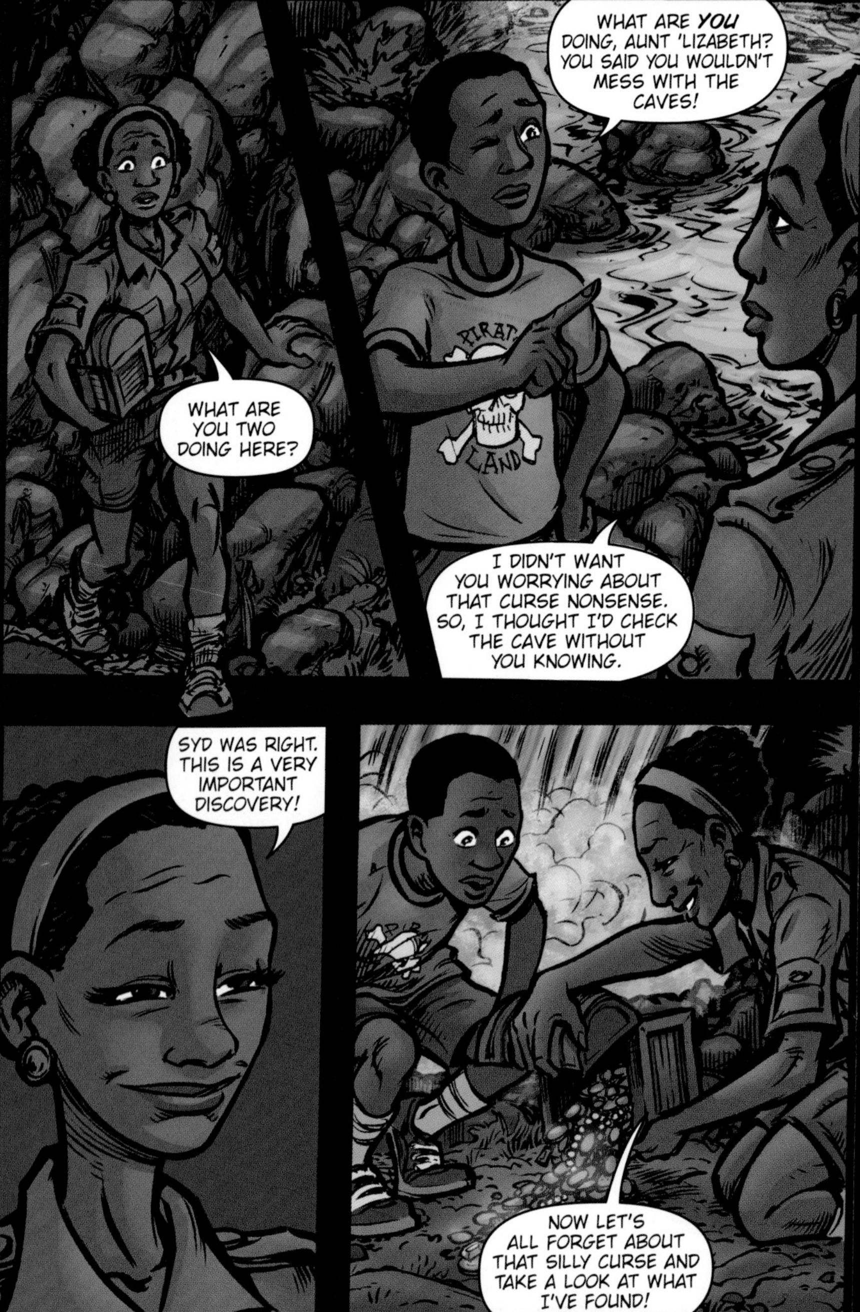
WHAT ARE YOU TWO DOING HERE?
WHAT ARE ***YOU*** DOING, AUNT 'LIZABETH? YOU SAID YOU WOULDN'T MESS WITH THE CAVES!
PIRATE LAND
I DIDN'T WANT YOU WORRYING ABOUT THAT CURSE NONSENSE. SO, I THOUGHT I'D CHECK THE CAVE WITHOUT YOU KNOWING.
SYD WAS RIGHT. THIS IS A VERY IMPORTANT DISCOVERY!
NOW LET'S ALL FORGET ABOUT THAT SILLY CURSE AND TAKE A LOOK AT WHAT I'VE FOUND!

GO ON TO THE NEXT PAGE.

You and Jimmy sit down by Dr Chase as she shows you the treasure. She explains where the coins came from and shows you diamonds, rubies and emeralds.

After several minutes, you hear someone in the trees.

'Here come Syd and Marty,' says Dr Chase. 'They must have been frantic when they realized you were gone!'

But it's not Syd and Marty.

A large group of people stagger into the clearing, wearing torn and dirty clothes. They have blank, white eyes and yellow teeth fill their slack jaws.

They aren't people at all . . .

'Zombies!' Jimmy howls. He starts to scoop up the coins and jewels, screaming, 'We'll put it back!'

Maybe putting it back will make them stop!

Then Dr Chase picks up the wooden chest and smashes it over the head of a zombie that was trying to grab Jimmy. Treasure spills out everywhere.

The zombie grabs her instead.

Then another one grabs you . . .

THE END

'Maybe we'd better get to the lagoon!' you say. 'What if . . . uh . . . Dylan convinces the captain to leave without us? We'd be stranded.'

After a little discussion, Syd decides that you're right and gets everyone running down the path to the lagoon.

After a couple minutes, Marty begs you all to wait. 'I . . . *huff, huff* . . . have to . . . *huff* . . . catch my breath,' he says. He bends over, hands on his knees, breathing hard.

You pull on his arm. 'Come on,' you say. 'It's not much further!'

Marty shakes off your hand. 'This is all ridiculous. I'm sure Dylan isn't going to run off on us.'

'He seemed pretty scared,' you say.

'He's been scared since we got here!' says Jimmy. 'Anyway, I'm tired too. We walked all over the island this morning. Let's take a break?'

GO ON TO THE NEXT PAGE.

WILL YOU ...

... keep going?
TURN TO PAGE 10.

... take a break?
TURN TO PAGE 34.

When you wake up Dr Chase, she wakes everyone else to see who's missing. It's the captain!

'Do you have any clue what he's up to?' she asks Dylan.

'Not unless he's after Bloody Bob's treasure,' Dylan replies.

Dr Chase laughs. 'I heard you telling that story to the kids earlier. I can't believe the captain would go chasing after some old legend.'

Still, she decides to follow his trail and see where he went. You and Jimmy want to go too, but she tells you to stay with Syd and Marty.

'They'll probably just sneak after you anyway,' says Dylan. 'I'll come along and keep an eye on them.'

'You're probably right,' says Dr Chase. 'All right, then. What harm can there be?'

Quietly, Dylan tells you and Jimmy to bring your salt with you.

GO ON TO THE NEXT PAGE.

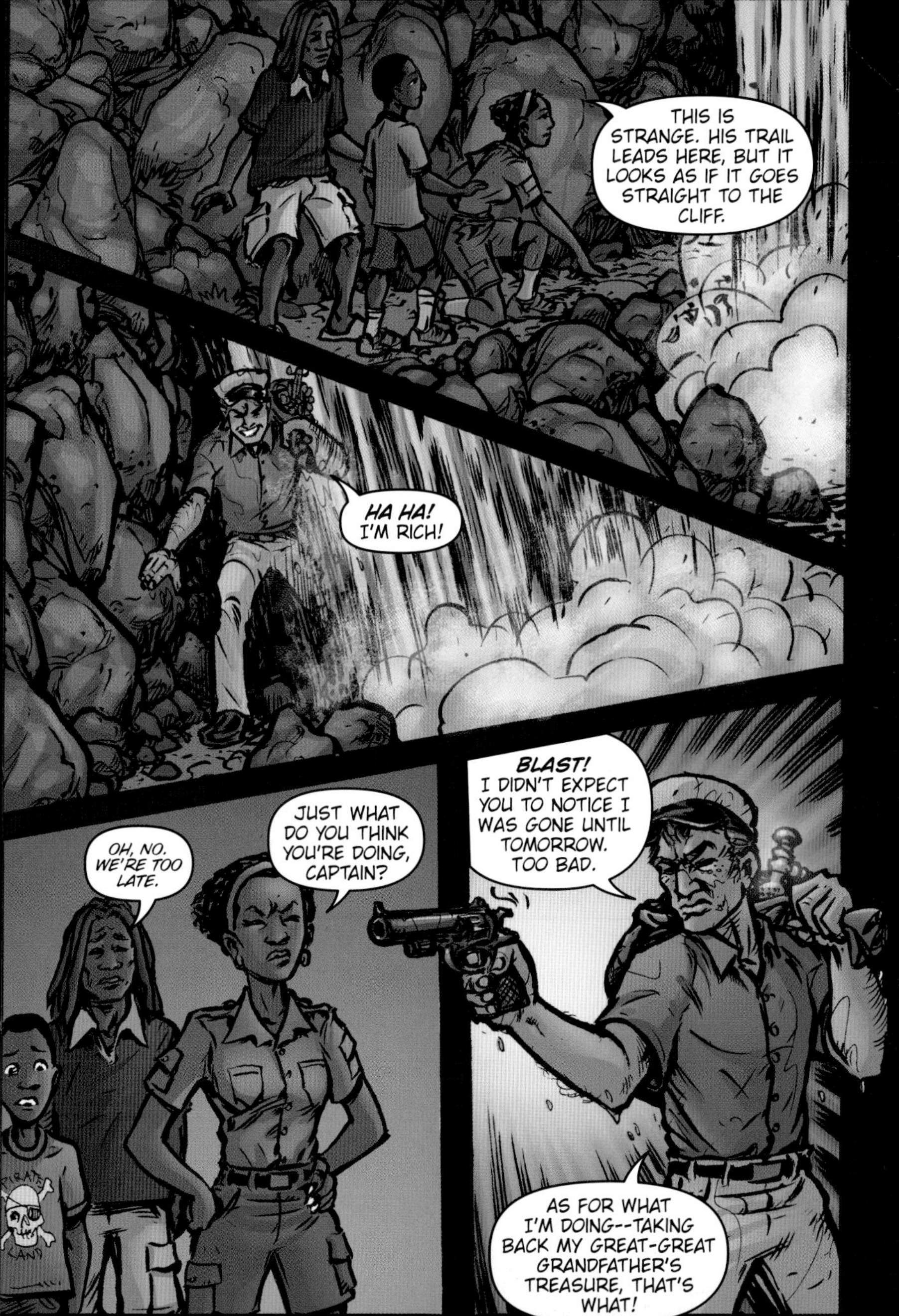
THIS IS STRANGE. HIS TRAIL LEADS HERE, BUT IT LOOKS AS IF IT GOES STRAIGHT TO THE CLIFF.
HA HA! I'M RICH!
OH, NO. WE'RE TOO LATE.
JUST WHAT DO YOU THINK YOU'RE DOING, CAPTAIN?
BLAST! I DIDN'T EXPECT YOU TO NOTICE I WAS GONE UNTIL TOMORROW. TOO BAD.
AS FOR WHAT I'M DOING--TAKING BACK MY GREAT-GREAT GRANDFATHER'S TREASURE, THAT'S WHAT!

GO ON TO THE NEXT PAGE.

'The family always knew he hid it behind a waterfall on some island,' he laughs. 'We just didn't know which one. But once you started looking for a charter boat to hire, Dylan there told me the zombie legend!'

Furious, Dylan grabs the captain. 'Idiot! You've killed us all!'

Startled, the captain doesn't shoot. Instead, he cracks Dylan across the side of his head with the pistol.

As Dylan crumples to the ground, Dr Chase starts towards him. The captain swings his pistol her way. 'Ah, ah, ah,' he says. 'After I'm gone.'

Staggering a little under the weight of his sack full of treasure, the captain disappears into the shadows under the trees.

Dr Chase kneels down beside Dylan to make sure he's okay. Then she turns towards you and says, 'The two of you run back to the camp. Ask Syd and Marty to radio for help!'

GO ON TO THE NEXT PAGE.

As you start towards camp, Jimmy stops and says, 'I bet we could get to the lagoon before the captain. He's moving pretty slowly with that bag full of stuff. We could hide the motorboat so he can't get to the *Marlin*! What do you say?'

WILL YOU ...

... go back to camp like Dr Chase said?
TURN TO PAGE 50.

... try to stop the captain from getting away?
TURN TO PAGE 82.

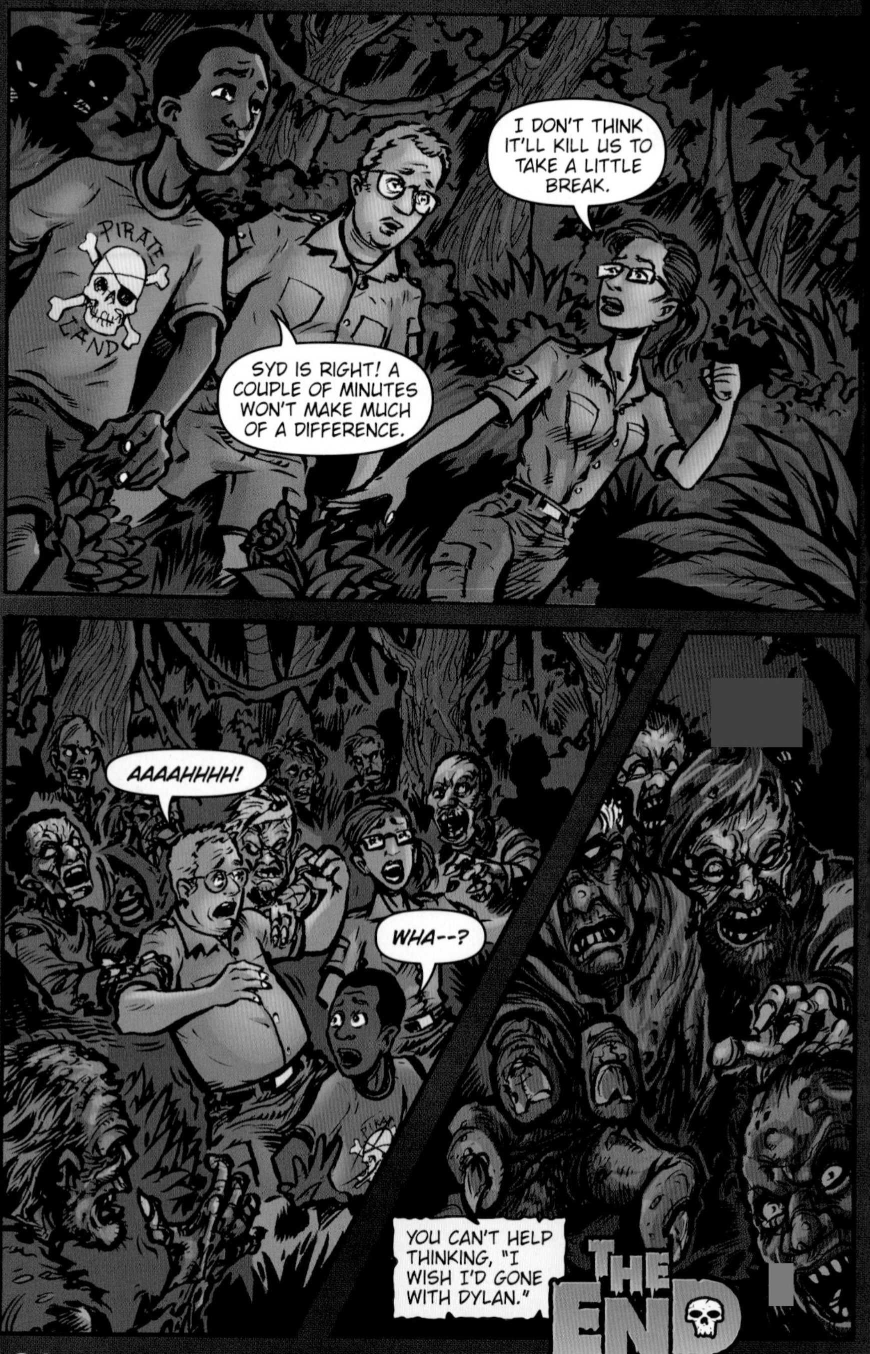
PIRATE CAND
I DON'T THINK IT'LL KILL US TO TAKE A LITTLE BREAK.
SYD IS RIGHT! A COUPLE OF MINUTES WON'T MAKE MUCH OF A DIFFERENCE.
AAAAHHHH!
WHA--?
YOU CAN'T HELP THINKING, "I WISH I'D GONE WITH DYLAN."
THE END

'Let's see where he's going,' you say.

'How do you know it's a he?' Jimmy asks.

'He, she, whatever,' you reply. 'C'mon!'

The two of you slip out into the night. You keep your torches off so the light doesn't give you away.

Between the dark and being so tired from your explorations that morning, you both stumble a few times on roots and rocks. Fortunately, the person you're following doesn't seem to hear you.

You come to the clearing by the waterfall and hide behind some plants at the edge. The pale moonlight reveals that you've been following . . . Dylan!

He walks towards the waterfall and slips under it into the cave.

'What's he doing?' Jimmy whispers. You shrug, just as confused as he is.

'I thought he didn't want us messing with the cave or the treasure,' you say softly.

'What should we do?' Jimmy whispers.

GO ON TO THE NEXT PAGE.

WILL YOU . . .

. . . go back to camp and tell Dr Chase?
TURN TO PAGE 45.

. . . wait outside until Dylan comes out?
TURN TO PAGE 48.

. . . follow him inside?
TURN TO PAGE 66.

'I'll go and get him,' you say.

Dr Chase is worried you might get lost, but you tell her you can just follow the stream down to the lagoon. Finally, she says okay.

As you hurry towards the beach, you hear noises back in the trees. You shine your torch. Someone is there!

'Dylan?' you call softly. 'Is that you?'

A low moan is your only reply. Then a little old woman in a tattered dress steps into the beam of your torch. She reaches for you with hands twisted like claws.

She's a zombie!

You turn and run, but not before you see others behind her.

They're still following you when you reach the lagoon.

You see Dylan, waiting like he promised he would. He starts the engine as you dive into the motorboat.

As it pulls away from the shore, you realize that you're the only ones who will escape from Zombie Island.

THE END

WILL YOU . . .

. . . agree with Syd?
TURN TO PAGE 41.

. . . try to talk Dylan out of
whatever he's doing?
TURN TO PAGE 47.

You and Jimmy hurry over to Dr Chase's tent.

'Aunt 'Lizabeth!' Jimmy hisses. 'Wake up!'

Moments later, a bleary-eyed Dr Chase comes out. Covering a yawn with her hand, she asks what's wrong.

'We saw someone sneaking out of camp!' you reply.

'That's strange,' she says. 'Let's see who it was.'

Waking everyone else, she finds that Syd and Marty are there. So is Captain Allen.

'Where's Dylan?' she asks him. 'The cave, perhaps?'

'That doesn't make sense,' he replies. 'Dylan's been going on about that curse. Why would he go treasure-hunting in the middle of the night?'

'We should make sure,' Syd says. 'Let's check the cave!'

'It's probably not a good idea for all of us to start running around in the dark,' says Dr Chase. 'Perhaps we should just wait for him to come back.'

WILL YOU . . .

. . . wait for Dylan to come back?
TURN TO PAGE 57.

. . . go and check at the cave?
TURN TO PAGE 80.

Hoping to distract Dylan so that Syd and the captain can grab him, you charge right at him, screaming.

Your plan works! He jumps back, spilling the coins that were in his hand. While his attention is on you, the captain and Syd rush forwards.

In a few seconds, they wrestle him to the ground.

He starts to laugh.

'What so funny, crazy guy?' Syd asks.

'Tying me up won't help,' says Dylan. 'They're already coming.'

'Who?' snarls the captain. 'And don't give me any of this zombie nonsense!'

'You'll see soon enough,' Dylan replies as the captain drags him to his feet.

As you walk back towards the camp, you hear something coming through the trees. Zombies lurch slowly out of the shadows, moaning and grunting.

'Guess now you'll believe me,' Dylan says, smiling sadly.

THE END

'Let's just paddle!' you yell. 'They're almost here!'

Dylan takes one paddle, and Jimmy grabs the other. Dr Chase keeps working the engine, but it does nothing more than splutter.

You see the zombies emerge from the shadows beneath the trees and scream for the others to hurry!

Jimmy digs too deep with his paddle and loses his grip. Trying to grab it, he slips into the water. Dr Chase leaves the engine and dives in after him. Dylan, worried about leaving them behind, stops paddling.

A hand gropes for a grip on the motorboat. You reach out, thinking it's Jimmy or Dr Chase. As soon as it grabs you, you know it's not.

The cold, cold hand pulls you into the water. You splash and struggle, until a mouth filled with yellow teeth opens wide and bites down . . .

THE END

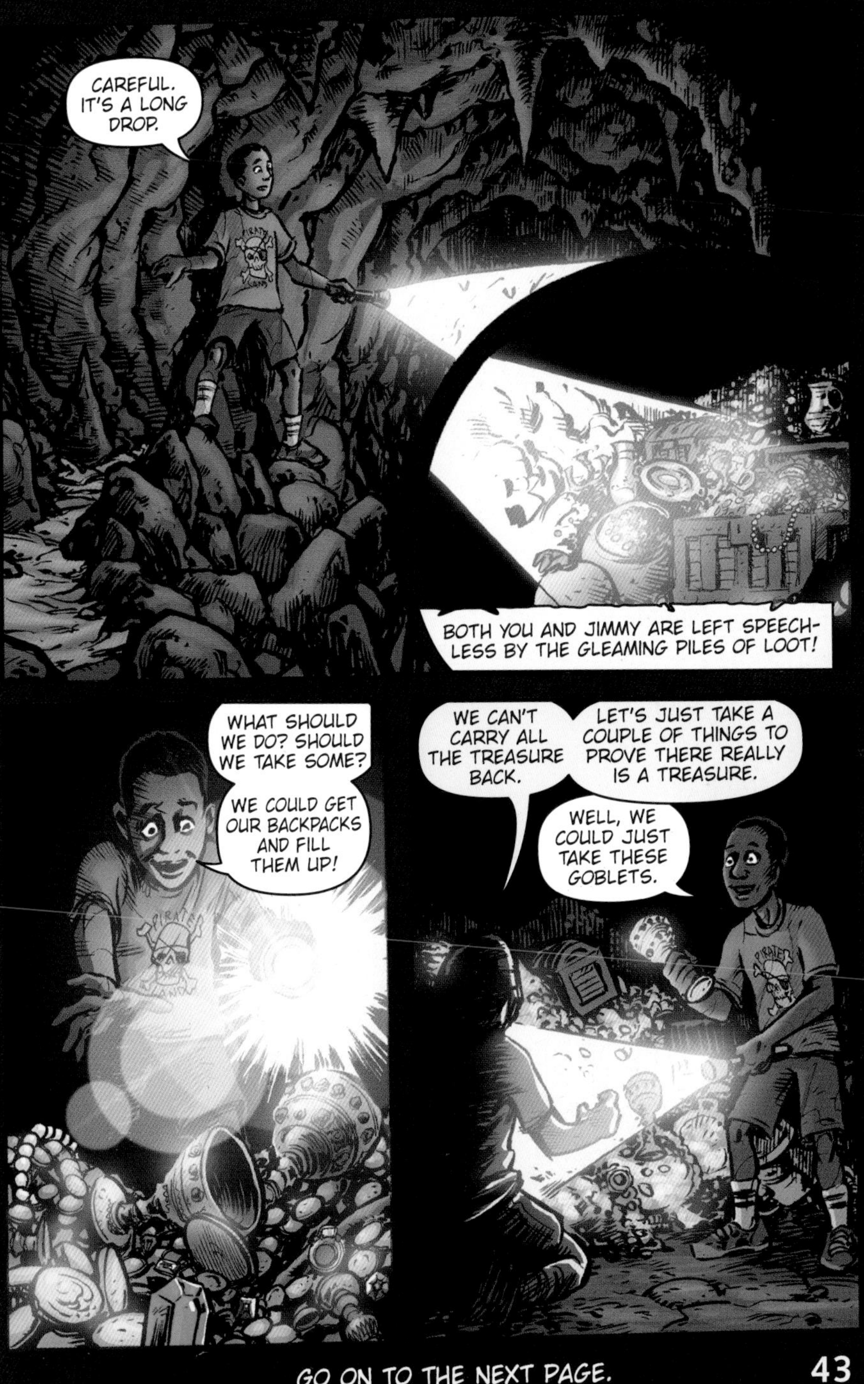
CAREFUL. IT'S A LONG DROP.
BOTH YOU AND JIMMY ARE LEFT SPEECHLESS BY THE GLEAMING PILES OF LOOT!
WHAT SHOULD WE DO? SHOULD WE TAKE SOME?
WE COULD GET OUR BACKPACKS AND FILL THEM UP!
WE CAN'T CARRY ALL THE TREASURE BACK.
LET'S JUST TAKE A COUPLE OF THINGS TO PROVE THERE REALLY IS A TREASURE.
WELL, WE COULD JUST TAKE THESE GOBLETS.

GO ON TO THE NEXT PAGE.

WILL YOU . . .

... fill your backpacks with treasure?
TURN TO PAGE 63.

... take the goblets to show everyone
that the treasure is real?
TURN TO PAGE 91.

Rushing back to camp, you shout and scream until everyone is awake. Gasping for air, you try to tell Dr Chase what's happening.

'Dylan . . . ' you start.

'The cave . . . ' says Jimmy.

When you finally finish, Dr Chase turns to the captain.

'What's he up to?' she asks.

'I'm not sure,' he says. 'Maybe that curse stuff was just a trick! Maybe he was after the treasure all along!'

'That makes more sense than a curse,' says Dr Chase.

'We'd better get to the lagoon!' exclaims the captain. 'He might try to steal the *Marlin* and strand us here!'

As the captain runs off, Dr Chase says, 'Come on, everyone. We should stick together until we find out what's going on!'

When you get to the lagoon, the captain is standing by the motorboat, breathing heavily. 'No . . . sign . . . yet,' he gasps.

Suddenly, his eyes go wide. He points behind you, shouting, 'Look!'

GO ON TO THE NEXT PAGE.

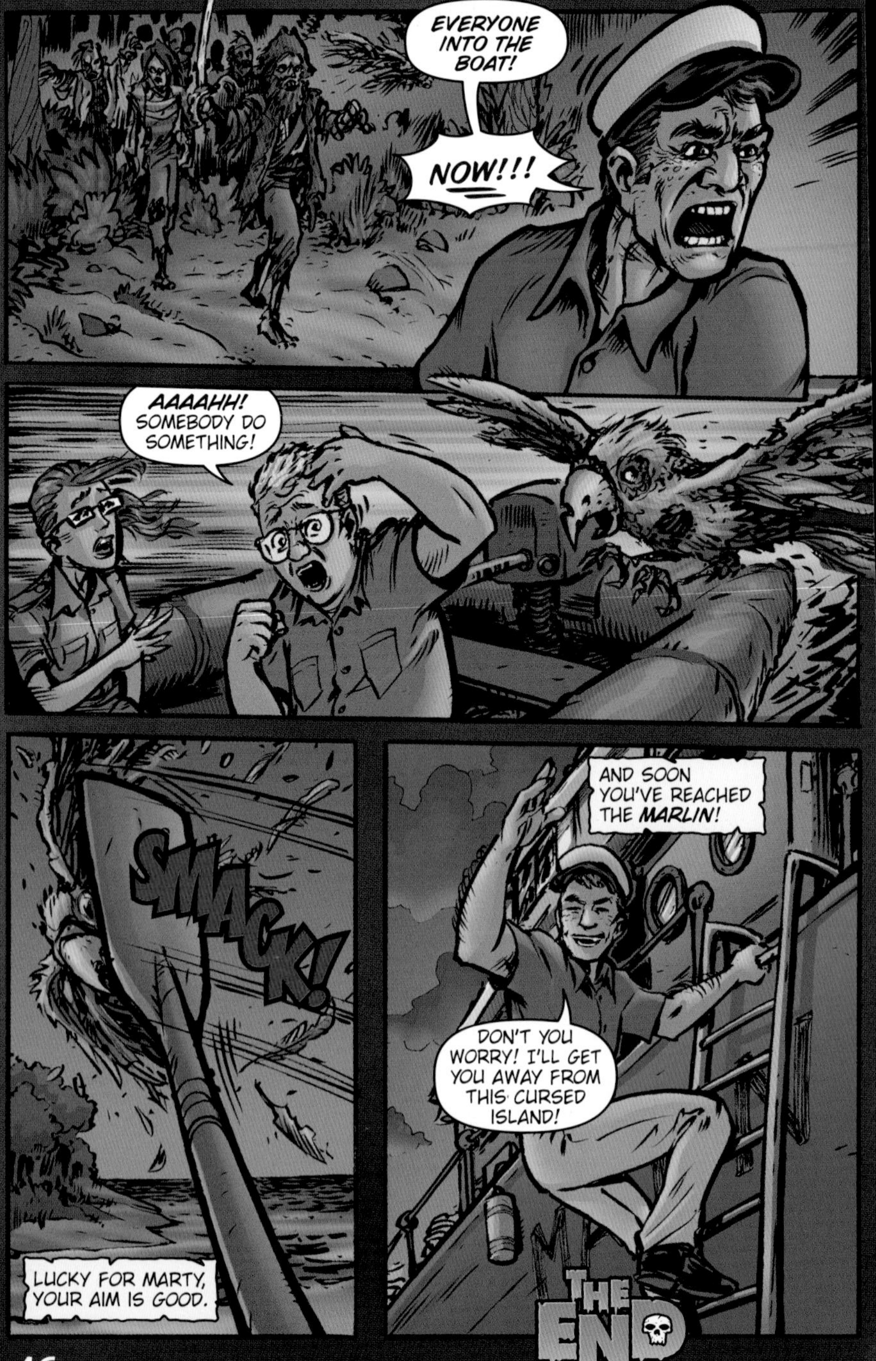
EVERYONE INTO THE BOAT!
NOW!!!
AAAAHH! SOMEBODY DO SOMETHING!
SMACK!
LUCKY FOR MARTY, YOUR AIM IS GOOD.
AND SOON YOU'VE REACHED THE MARLIN!
DON'T YOU WORRY! I'LL GET YOU AWAY FROM THIS CURSED ISLAND!
THE END

'If there really is a curse,' you say to Dylan, 'then aren't you just doing what you said we'd do? Dragging your dead relatives out of their graves?'

'But for one last time,' he whispers.

'How do you know?' you say. 'People will come looking for us. Or someone else might find this place by accident.'

'It has to stop,' he says. 'It has to!'

'Maybe Dr Chase can help. She's famous! If you prove the curse is real, she can help to stop people from coming here,' you say.

'Would you?' he asks Dr Chase.

'I don't believe in curses,' she says, 'but – '

Dylan points behind her. There are zombies coming out from under the trees!

'Yes!' Dr Chase screams. 'I'll help!'

Dylan leaps back through the waterfall. Inside the cave, you hear coins ringing on the stone floor.

Amazed, you watch the zombies turn and shuffle back into the shadows! Once you leave here, you'll all make sure no one else ever comes searching for the cursed treasure!

THE END

'Let's stay here until he comes out,' you whisper.

'Okay,' he says.

As you wait, you can't help yawning. Your eyelids feel heavy.

Plunk! A loud noise wakes you.

Plunk! Jimmy has fallen asleep too. You put your hand over his mouth and shake him. His eyes flick open. You put a finger to your lips and then point to the clearing.

Dylan has come back out of the cave. He's standing at the edge of the pool, tossing something into it.

A golden gleam catches your eye. He's tossing gold coins into the pool!

Treasure!

'He shouldn't be doing that,' Jimmy says.

He starts to get up, as if he's going to go talk to Dylan.

GO ON TO THE NEXT PAGE.

WILL YOU . . .

. . . confront Dylan?
TURN TO PAGE 70.

. . . go back and tell
Dr Chase what's happening?
TURN TO PAGE 100.

'Your aunt said to head for camp,' you say, grabbing Jimmy's arm. 'C'mon!'

When you get back to camp, you tell Syd and Marty what happened. While Marty is sputtering his confusion, Syd rushes to the radio.

'It's broken!' she groans. 'The captain must have messed with it!'

Marty is good with electronics, so he takes a look at it. 'I think I can fix it,' he says, 'but it'll take some time.'

Suddenly, a horrible scream echoes across the island!

Seconds later, Dr Chase and Dylan come crashing out of the darkness. Their eyes are full of fear.

'They're coming!' shouts Dr Chase.

50

GO ON TO THE NEXT PAGE.

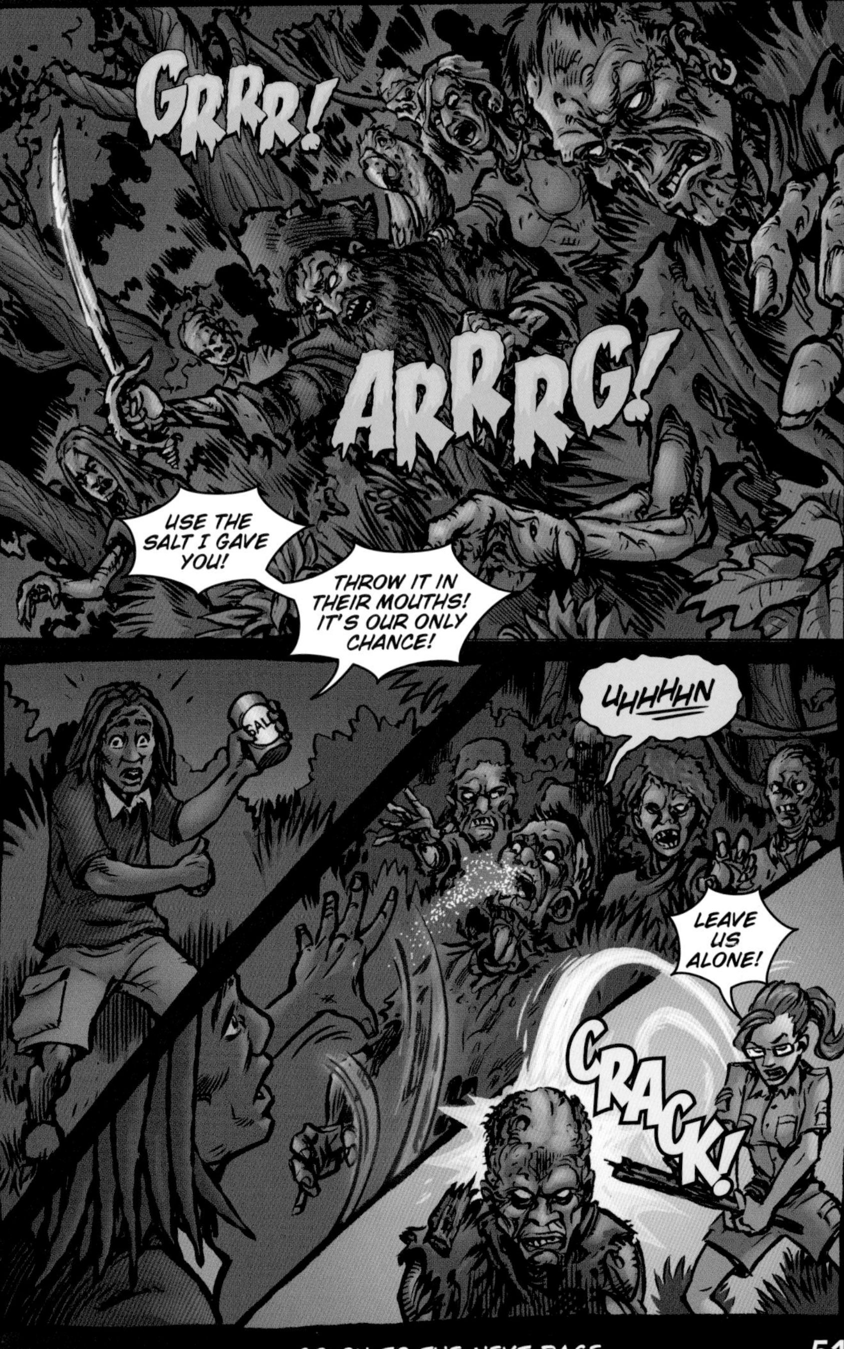
GRRR!
ARRRG!
USE THE SALT I GAVE YOU!
THROW IT IN THEIR MOUTHS! IT'S OUR ONLY CHANCE!
SALT
UHHHHN
LEAVE US ALONE!
CRACK!

GO ON TO THE NEXT PAGE.

You throw salt into the mouth of a zombie. It tumbles to the ground!

Then you hear screaming and see Syd mobbed by zombies and dragged down. Marty shouts her name and tries to run to her, but Dr Chase pulls him back.

'We have to try for the *Marlin*!' shouts Dylan.

'No!' yells Dr Chase. 'It could be gone already. Besides, we'll never get past them all.'

'We need to get into the house!' screams Marty. 'Barricade ourselves in where they can't get us!'

'No!' Dylan hollers. 'They'll keep coming until everyone on the island is dead! We have to get away. The *Marlin* will still be there. That first scream was the captain!'

GO ON TO THE NEXT PAGE.

WILL YOU . . .

. . . agree that Dylan is right and you have to get off the island?
TURN TO PAGE 71.

. . . agree that Marty is right and you can hold off the zombies from inside the house?
TURN TO PAGE 104.

You and Jimmy struggle to put on your backpacks and hurry to the camp. When you get there, the others have set up a group of tents in front of the crumbling plantation house.

Dumping your backpacks, you run over to Dr Chase. 'We found a secret cave!' Jimmy exclaims. 'It's behind a waterfall!'

Dr Chase gives him a frown. 'That's funny. I don't remember any waterfalls near the beach. Where have you kids been wandering off to?'

'Maybe it's the cave where the pirate hid his treasure,' you add. 'Like Dylan said. Guarded by a zombie curse!'

Dr Chase's eyes light up. 'Bloody Bob's treasure?' she gasps. 'That would be an amazing historical find! Think of the publicity! Can you two show me where it is?'

Alarmed, Dylan grabs her by the arm. 'Don't go!' he says. 'Nothing can be taken from those caves! The curse . . .'

'I don't believe in curses.' She laughs.

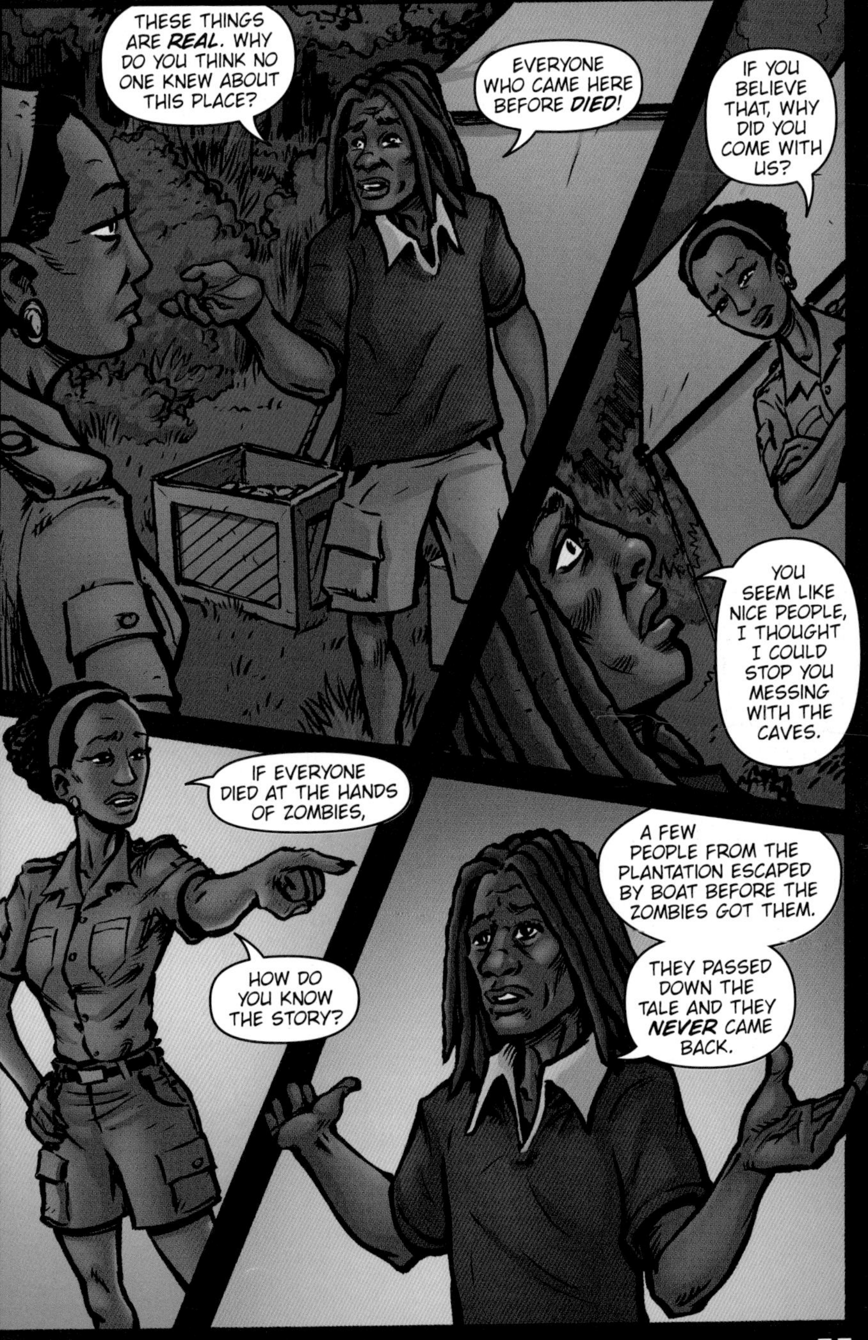
THESE THINGS ARE REAL. WHY DO YOU THINK NO ONE KNEW ABOUT THIS PLACE?
EVERYONE WHO CAME HERE BEFORE DIED!
IF YOU BELIEVE THAT, WHY DID YOU COME WITH US?
YOU SEEM LIKE NICE PEOPLE, I THOUGHT I COULD STOP YOU MESSING WITH THE CAVES.
IF EVERYONE DIED AT THE HANDS OF ZOMBIES,
HOW DO YOU KNOW THE STORY?
A FEW PEOPLE FROM THE PLANTATION ESCAPED BY BOAT BEFORE THE ZOMBIES GOT THEM.
THEY PASSED DOWN THE TALE AND THEY NEVER CAME BACK.

GO ON TO THE NEXT PAGE.

WILL YOU ...

... decide Dylan might be
right about the curse?
TURN TO PAGE 12.

... be silent and trust Dr Chase to make
the best decision?
TURN TO PAGE 8.

... agree with Dr Chase
that Dylan is just being superstitious?
TURN TO PAGE 76.

'Maybe we should just wait,' you say. 'Besides, we don't even know that he went to the cave!'

'No,' says Dr Chase. 'We don't. Why don't the rest of you go back to sleep. I think I'll wait up and talk to Dylan when he gets back.'

You try to fall back asleep, but you can't. Neither can Jimmy.

'What do you think Dylan is doing?' you ask him.

'I don't know,' Jimmy says. 'He seems nice, though. I don't think he'd do anything bad.'

Just then, you hear Dr Chase screaming!

You throw open your tent to see what's wrong.

A group of people are coming out from under the trees. Their clothes are dirty and falling apart. They look like pirates! A big man with a red beard holding a sword is leading them.

'Bloody Bob!' you whisper.

'Zombies!' gasps Jimmy.

It looks as if you're both right.

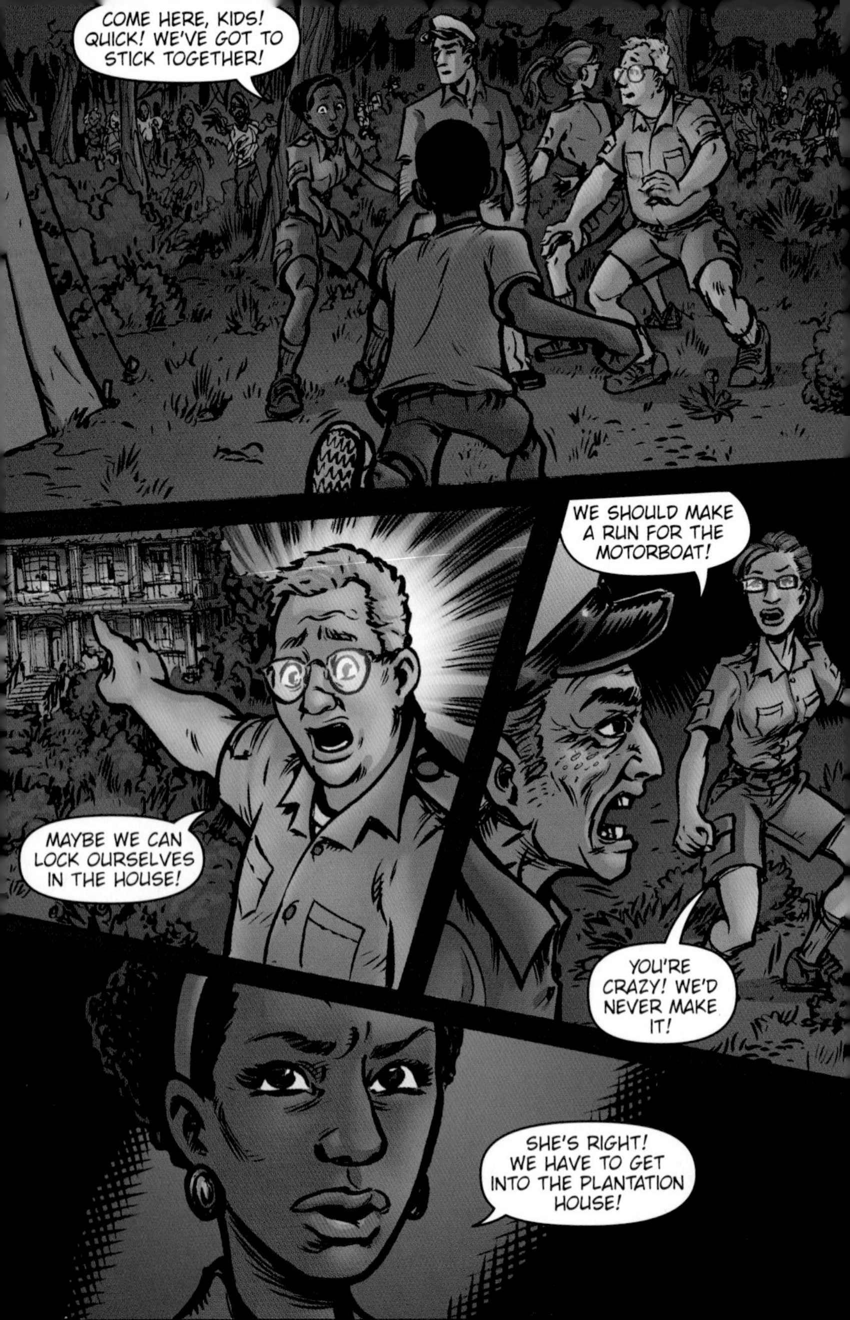
COME HERE, KIDS! QUICK! WE'VE GOT TO STICK TOGETHER!
MAYBE WE CAN LOCK OURSELVES IN THE HOUSE!
WE SHOULD MAKE A RUN FOR THE MOTORBOAT!
YOU'RE CRAZY! WE'D NEVER MAKE IT!
SHE'S RIGHT! WE HAVE TO GET INTO THE PLANTATION HOUSE!

GO ON TO THE NEXT PAGE

The captain shouts, 'Forget that! I'm making a run for it!'

As you head for the plantation house, you glance back. You see the big red-bearded pirate lurch in front of the captain. The captain grabs the zombie's arm, trying to wrestle away its sword.

You turn away as you get to the front steps of the house. They look rickety, but you saw Syd, Marty, and Dr Chase use them earlier. They should hold.

Jimmy charges up the stairs ahead of you.

Behind you, the captain starts to howl in pain.

You put your hands to your ears and keep running.

You don't even notice that Jimmy has stopped just inside the front door. He cries, 'Look out!' but you can't stop. You crash into him.

The two of you topple forwards into a huge hole in the front hallway floor.

You both scream as you fall.

THE END

You grab your torches and follow the shadowy figure. Jimmy almost turns his on, but you warn him that will make you too easy to see.

Just then, a torch switches on ahead of you. It makes following easier, but it's hard to keep up without making too much noise.

After what seems like forever, you come to a clearing. In the pale moonlight, you can finally see who was ahead of you – Captain Allen!

There's a short cliff at the back of the clearing, with a waterfall tumbling over it into a small pool. Still hidden, you watch the captain make his way to the cliff.

He scrambles out onto a ledge just a little above the water. Then he disappears, through the waterfall!

'What's he doing?' Jimmy whispers.

You shrug. 'Maybe there's a cave in there. Maybe he's after the pirate treasure!'

'What should we do?' Jimmy asks.

WILL YOU . . .

. . . wait until the captain comes out?
TURN TO PAGE 109.

. . . go in after him?
TURN TO PAGE 90.

. . . go back to camp and
tell the others?
TURN TO PAGE 78.

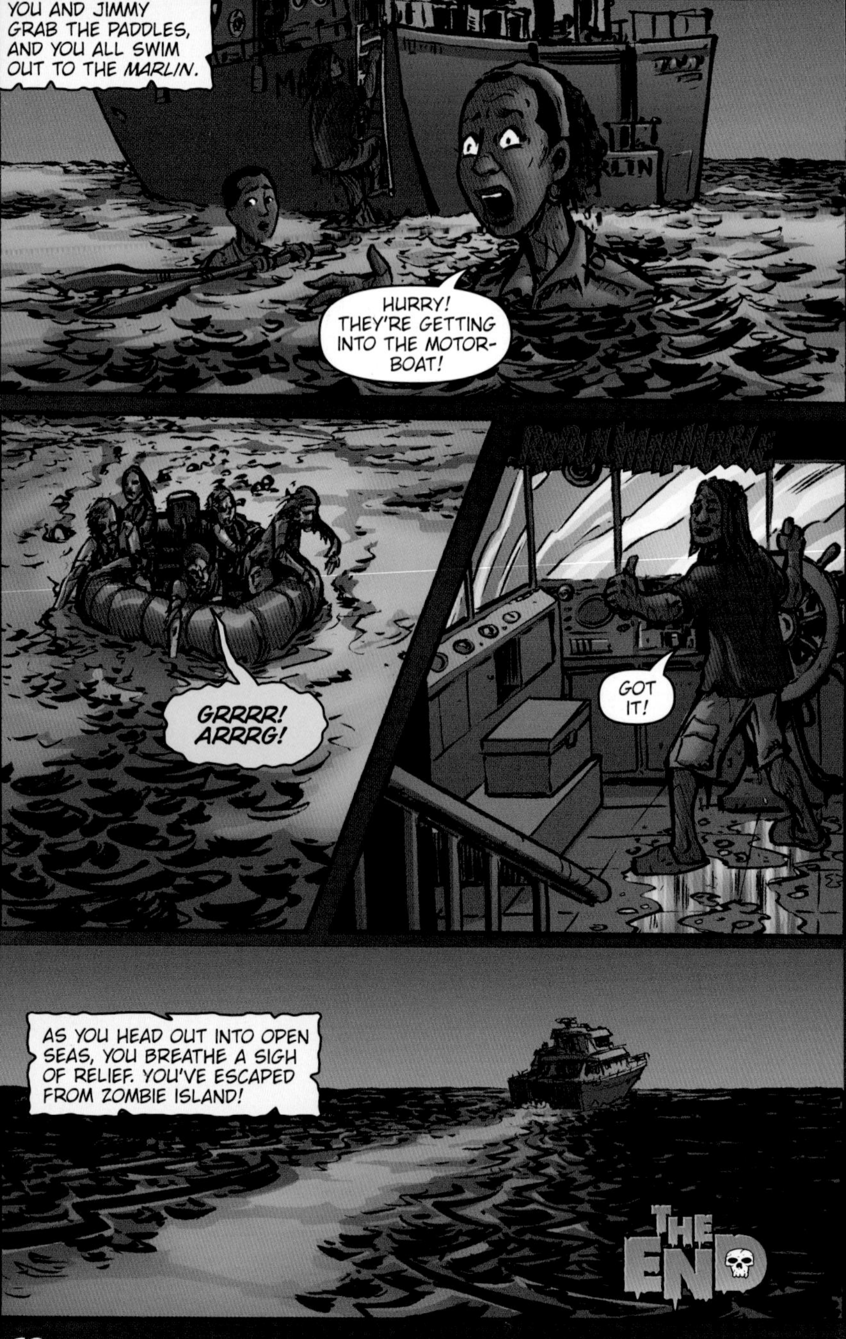
YOU AND JIMMY GRAB THE PADDLES, AND YOU ALL SWIM OUT TO THE *MARLIN*.
HURRY! THEY'RE GETTING INTO THE MOTOR-BOAT!
GRRRR! ARRRG!
GOT IT!
AS YOU HEAD OUT INTO OPEN SEAS, YOU BREATHE A SIGH OF RELIEF. YOU'VE ESCAPED FROM ZOMBIE ISLAND!
THE END

You decide that Jimmy is right. The two of you go and get your backpacks. You empty them out and go back inside.

Mostly, you fill them with coins, but you put in some jewellery too. Jimmy takes a goblet he was looking at, so you grab one for yourself.

The bags are really heavy and awkward when they're full. You have to crawl along the ledge, past the big drop, because you can't hug the wall with the backpacks on.

As you duck back through the waterfall, you feel a shiver run down your spine. Probably just from getting soaked for a third time.

You and Jimmy collapse on the ground outside, breathing hard.

'Treasure sure is heavy,' gasps Jimmy. 'Maybe we should get some help.'

'Do you think your aunt will let us keep it?' you ask.

Jimmy frowns. 'I don't know. She'll probably say it's historical or something. Maybe we should bury it?'

GO ON TO THE NEXT PAGE.

WILL YOU . . .

. . . haul it all back to show Dr Chase?
TURN TO PAGE 89.

. . . go and get help to bring
the treasure to camp?
TURN TO PAGE 67.

. . . bury the treasure?
TURN TO PAGE 103.

As the zombies lurch your way, you throw a handful of salt at the one in front. It stumbles and drops to the ground!

Cheering you on, Jimmy joins in.

You dodge through the trees, throwing salt whenever the zombies get too close. Before long, you get to the beach.

The zombies aren't far behind.

'I'll hold them off!' you yell to Jimmy. 'Get the engine started!'

As the zombies shamble out onto the sand, Jimmy leaps into the motorboat. You pour some salt into your hand.

You yell for Jimmy to hurry as you throw salt at the first zombie that comes close.

'I can't make it work!' Jimmy wails.

You tilt the salt pot to pour some more into your hand. Empty!

Icy fingers grab hold of you. You drop the empty salt pot to the ground. You struggle to break free, but the zombies are too strong . . .

THE END

'We've come this far,' you say. 'Let's go after him!'

'Okay.' Jimmy yawns.

You hurry across the clearing and slip through the water-fall into the space beyond. The water is cold. You shiver.

You don't hear anything, so you turn on your torches.

Jimmy starts to moves quietly down the tunnel. You follow.

Before long, the tunnel opens into a larger space with a deep crevice. The only way to the other side is a narrow ledge.

As Jimmy eases out onto the ledge, you whisper, 'Be careful.'

It doesn't help. Tired and careless, Jimmy slips in the water dripping off of him.

You dive forwards onto your stomach, reaching for his hand. You just barely grab on.

His weight is enough to pull you down along with him.

You drop into darkness, watching Jimmy fall below you, lit by the flickering torches that tumble down with you . . .

THE END

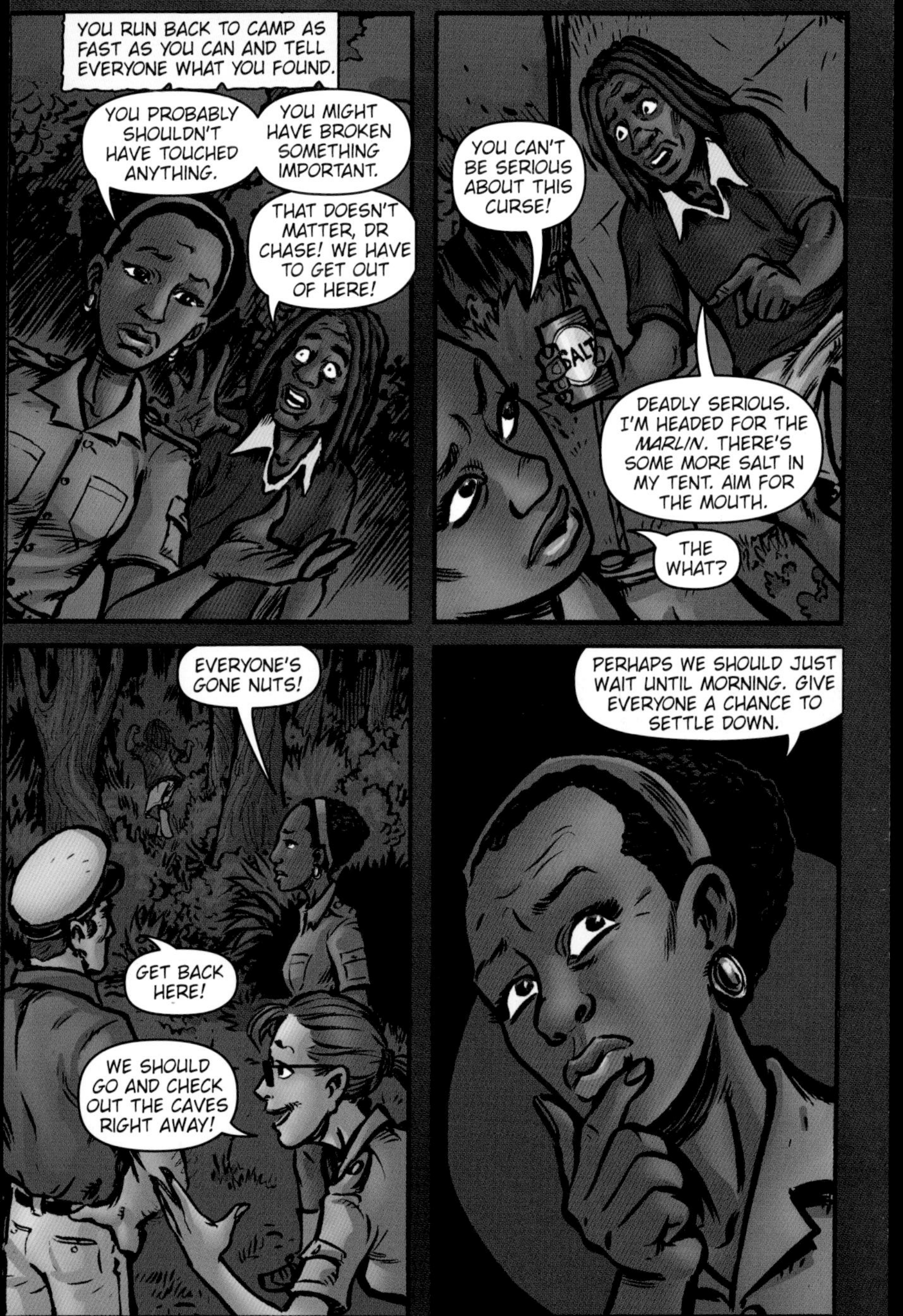
YOU RUN BACK TO CAMP AS FAST AS YOU CAN AND TELL EVERYONE WHAT YOU FOUND.
YOU PROBABLY SHOULDN'T HAVE TOUCHED ANYTHING.
YOU MIGHT HAVE BROKEN SOMETHING IMPORTANT.
THAT DOESN'T MATTER, DR CHASE! WE HAVE TO GET OUT OF HERE!
YOU CAN'T BE SERIOUS ABOUT THIS CURSE!
SALT
DEADLY SERIOUS. I'M HEADED FOR THE *MARLIN*. THERE'S SOME MORE SALT IN MY TENT. AIM FOR THE MOUTH.
THE WHAT?
EVERYONE'S GONE NUTS!
GET BACK HERE!
WE SHOULD GO AND CHECK OUT THE CAVES RIGHT AWAY!
PERHAPS WE SHOULD JUST WAIT UNTIL MORNING. GIVE EVERYONE A CHANCE TO SETTLE DOWN.

GO ON TO THE NEXT PAGE.

WILL YOU . . .

. . . agree that Dr Chase is right
about waiting until morning?
TURN TO PAGE 74.

. . . go to the *Marlin* with Dylan?
TURN TO PAGE 85.

. . . volunteer to show Syd the treasure?
TURN TO PAGE 86.

You tell Dr Chase that you want to go to the *Marlin* with Dylan. After a second, Jimmy agrees.

'Happy now?' Dr Chase asks Dylan. 'You've frightened these poor children.'

He starts to reply, but she just tells him to take you and Jimmy and go. 'They can stay on the *Marlin* overnight. In the morning, they'll see how foolish you're being.'

Without a word, Dylan hurries you both towards the beach.

Before long, you hear something moving in the trees. Dylan screams, 'RUN!'

When you reach the beach, Dylan leaps into the motorboat to start the engine. You and Jimmy climb in as quick as you can.

Behind you, a bunch of people lurch onto the beach wearing tattered clothes and moaning softly.

'Zombies!' you and Jimmy gasp together.

The engine rumbles to life.

Soon, you are on the *Marlin*, sailing away from Zombie Island and thinking about the others who were left behind.

THE END

Jimmy rushes into the clearing and shouts, 'What are you doing!'

Dylan jumps with surprise. Then he looks sad. 'Oh, no. I was hoping you would all be asleep. It would be easier that way.'

'What do you mean?' you ask.

'My family came from this island,' he says. 'Only a few of them escaped from the pirates and zombies. Most didn't. Now, any time someone finds that cursed treasure, their rest is disturbed. That has to stop.'

'What are you talking about?' asks Jimmy.

Dylan smiles sadly. 'Once we all disappear, maybe people will finally leave the island alone.'

'Disappear?' you say. 'What – '

You're interrupted by the sound of someone coming into the clearing behind you. Turning, you see . . .

ZOMBIES!

'I tried to warn you all,' Dylan says sadly. 'You should never have come here.'

THE END

70

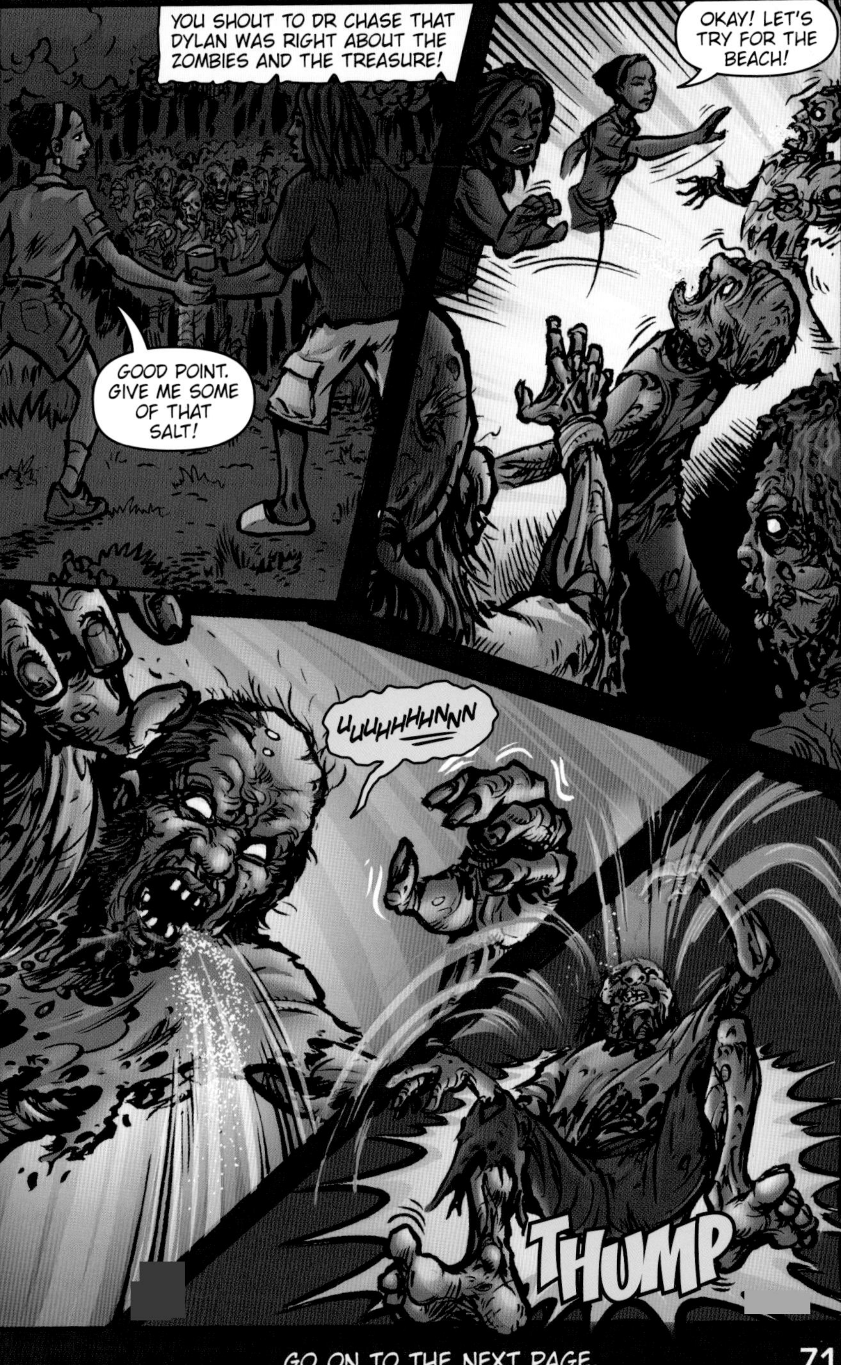
YOU SHOUT TO DR CHASE THAT DYLAN WAS RIGHT ABOUT THE ZOMBIES AND THE TREASURE!
GOOD POINT. GIVE ME SOME OF THAT SALT!
OKAY! LET'S TRY FOR THE BEACH!
UUUHHHHNNN
THUMP

GO ON TO THE NEXT PAGE.

Throwing handfuls of salt, the four of you manage to get past the pack of zombies and into the trees. As you run, you can hear them scrambling through the shadows behind you.

After a while, you pull ahead, certain you know exactly where the lagoon is. Suddenly, you trip!

The others arrive as you pick yourself up. That's when you realize what it is you tumbled over.

'Look!' you tell them. 'Captain Allen's bag! The treasure!'

Jimmy starts to ask, 'But where is . . . ' Then he notices the scraps of clothing scattered around the clearing. His hand shaking, he points to the captain's hat, trampled into the sand nearby.

Marty says, 'Maybe if we put the treasure back, they'll leave us alone!'

Dylan replies, 'If all they wanted was the treasure, they could have taken it after . . . when they were done with the captain. Let's keep going!'

GO ON TO THE NEXT PAGE.

WILL YOU . . .

. . . agree that Marty is right and you should try to take the treasure back to the cave?
TURN TO PAGE 94.

. . . agree that Dylan is right and you should just keep running?
TURN TO PAGE 106.

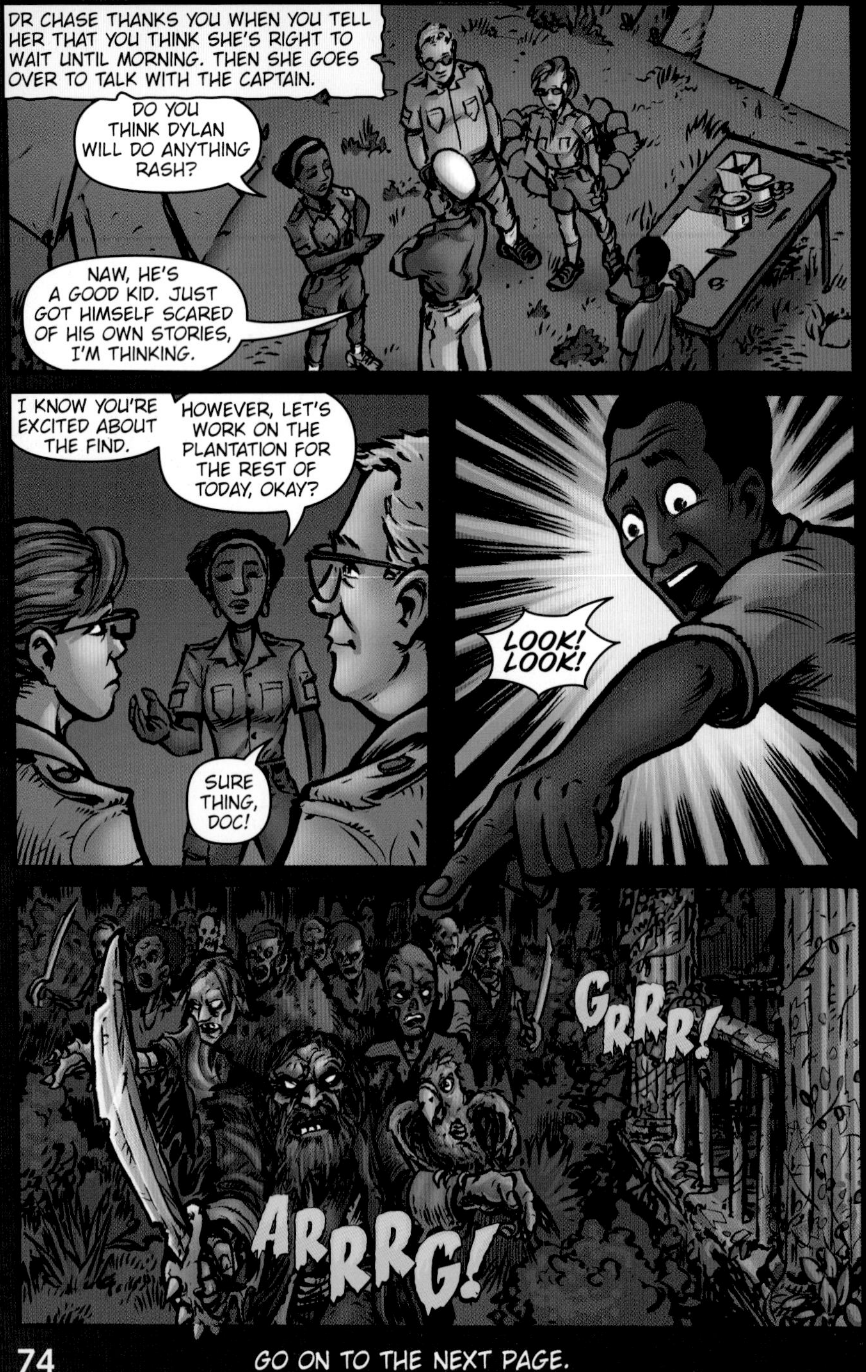
DR CHASE THANKS YOU WHEN YOU TELL HER THAT YOU THINK SHE'S RIGHT TO WAIT UNTIL MORNING. THEN SHE GOES OVER TO TALK WITH THE CAPTAIN.
DO YOU THINK DYLAN WILL DO ANYTHING RASH?
NAW, HE'S A GOOD KID. JUST GOT HIMSELF SCARED OF HIS OWN STORIES, I'M THINKING.
I KNOW YOU'RE EXCITED ABOUT THE FIND.
HOWEVER, LET'S WORK ON THE PLANTATION FOR THE REST OF TODAY, OKAY?
SURE THING, DOC!
LOOK! LOOK!
GRRRR!
ARRRG!

GO ON TO THE NEXT PAGE.

'What do we do?!' Jimmy yells.

'Salt!' you shout back. 'Dylan said to use salt!'

You remember he said there was some in his tent. As you run towards it, you see Syd pick up a camp shovel and swing it at one of the zombies.

Whack!

The zombie stops for a second, then reaches out for Syd.

Diving into Dylan's tent, you see several pots of salt tucked into one corner. Grabbing as many as you can, you scramble to the tent's mouth.

As you burst out, you crash into someone trying to get inside.

You both tumble to the ground, the salt pots rolling in every direction.

Jimmy moans, holding his head from smashing into yours. He doesn't even hear the zombie coming up behind him.

You scream for him to look out!

You don't even hear the zombie that comes up behind you . . .

THE END

'Dr Chase is right,' you tell Dylan. 'There's no such thing as a curse. Let's go and find the treasure!'

Everyone else agrees, but Dylan won't come.

'I'll wait at the lagoon,' he says. 'If something happens, run for the motorboat there.'

After he leaves, Dr Chase leaves Syd and Marty to watch the camp while you and Jimmy show her and the captain where to find the cave.

Once you get there, you duck under the waterfall and find a tunnel. You make your way through it, past a steep drop and into a larger cavern filled with pirate treasure!

'Amazing!' says Dr Chase. She examines a big jewel closely by the beam of her torch. 'Let's take as much as we can back to the camp so Syd, Marty and I can study it tonight.'

You can't help remembering how frightened Dylan was, though.

WILL YOU . . .

. . . have second thoughts about the curse?
TURN TO PAGE 96.

. . . take some treasure back to camp?
TURN TO PAGE 111.

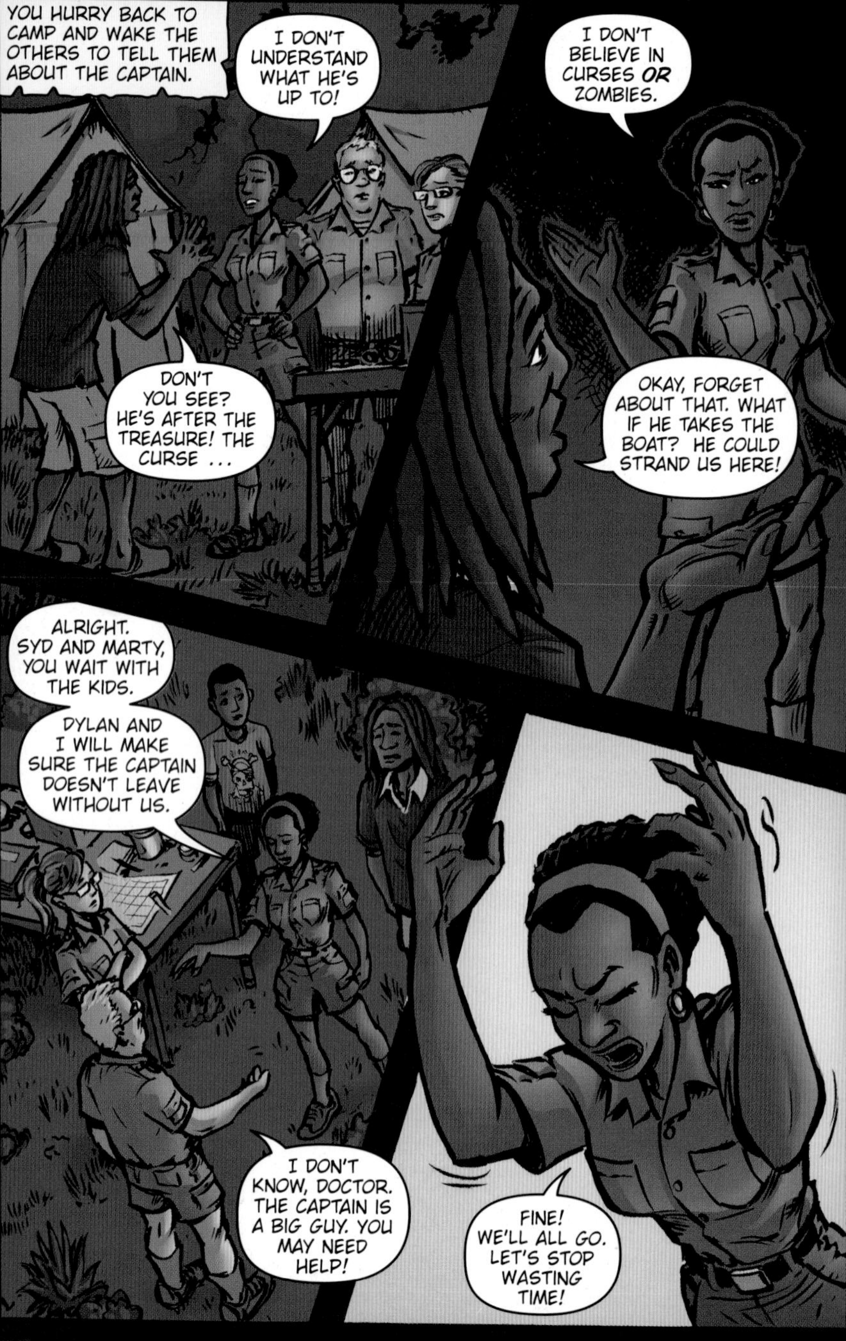
YOU HURRY BACK TO CAMP AND WAKE THE OTHERS TO TELL THEM ABOUT THE CAPTAIN.
I DON'T UNDERSTAND WHAT HE'S UP TO!
DON'T YOU SEE? HE'S AFTER THE TREASURE! THE CURSE . . .
I DON'T BELIEVE IN CURSES *OR* ZOMBIES.
OKAY, FORGET ABOUT THAT. WHAT IF HE TAKES THE BOAT? HE COULD STRAND US HERE!
ALRIGHT. SYD AND MARTY, YOU WAIT WITH THE KIDS.
DYLAN AND I WILL MAKE SURE THE CAPTAIN DOESN'T LEAVE WITHOUT US.
I DON'T KNOW, DOCTOR. THE CAPTAIN IS A BIG GUY. YOU MAY NEED HELP!
FINE! WE'LL ALL GO. LET'S STOP WASTING TIME!

GO ON TO THE NEXT PAGE.

All of you march down to the beach. Dylan jumps right into the motorboat and makes sure the engine is ready to start.

You wonder if the captain would really abandon you all there. He didn't seem like a bad guy.

After what seems like a long time, you hear someone coming towards you through the trees.

'Well, Captain,' Dr Chase calls out, 'what's going on . . . '

Her words die away as she sees what's coming out of the shadows.

ZOMBIES!

You hear the roar of the motorboat's engine behind you. 'Come on!' Dylan yells. 'Hurry!'

Barely believing what you're see- ing, all of you rush to climb into the motorboat.

The zombies plunge into the water behind you, but Dylan promises that he'll have the *Marlin* long gone before they can reach it.

'We'll be okay once we reach the open sea,' he says.

You hope that he's right.

THE END

'We can take you right to the cave,' you tell Syd. Jimmy agrees.

'Please, Dr Chase?' asks Syd. 'He could be disturbing an important historical find!'

'Okay,' says Dr Chase. 'We'll all go. Let's get some torches.'

With plenty of light, you and Jimmy have no trouble finding your way back to the clearing with the waterfall. When you arrive, there's no sign of Dylan.

'Maybe he didn't come here,' says Jimmy.

'Maybe he's already inside,' you reply. 'Should we go in?'

While everyone is deciding what to do, you see a shadow behind the waterfall.

You point and call out, 'Look!'

Just then, Dylan comes out of the waterfall. He's surprised to see you all there.

'What are you doing here, Dylan?' says Dr Chase.

Suddenly, Dylan looks angry for the first time since you met him.

'What am I doing here?' he yells. 'What are *you* doing here?'

GO ON TO THE NEXT PAGE.

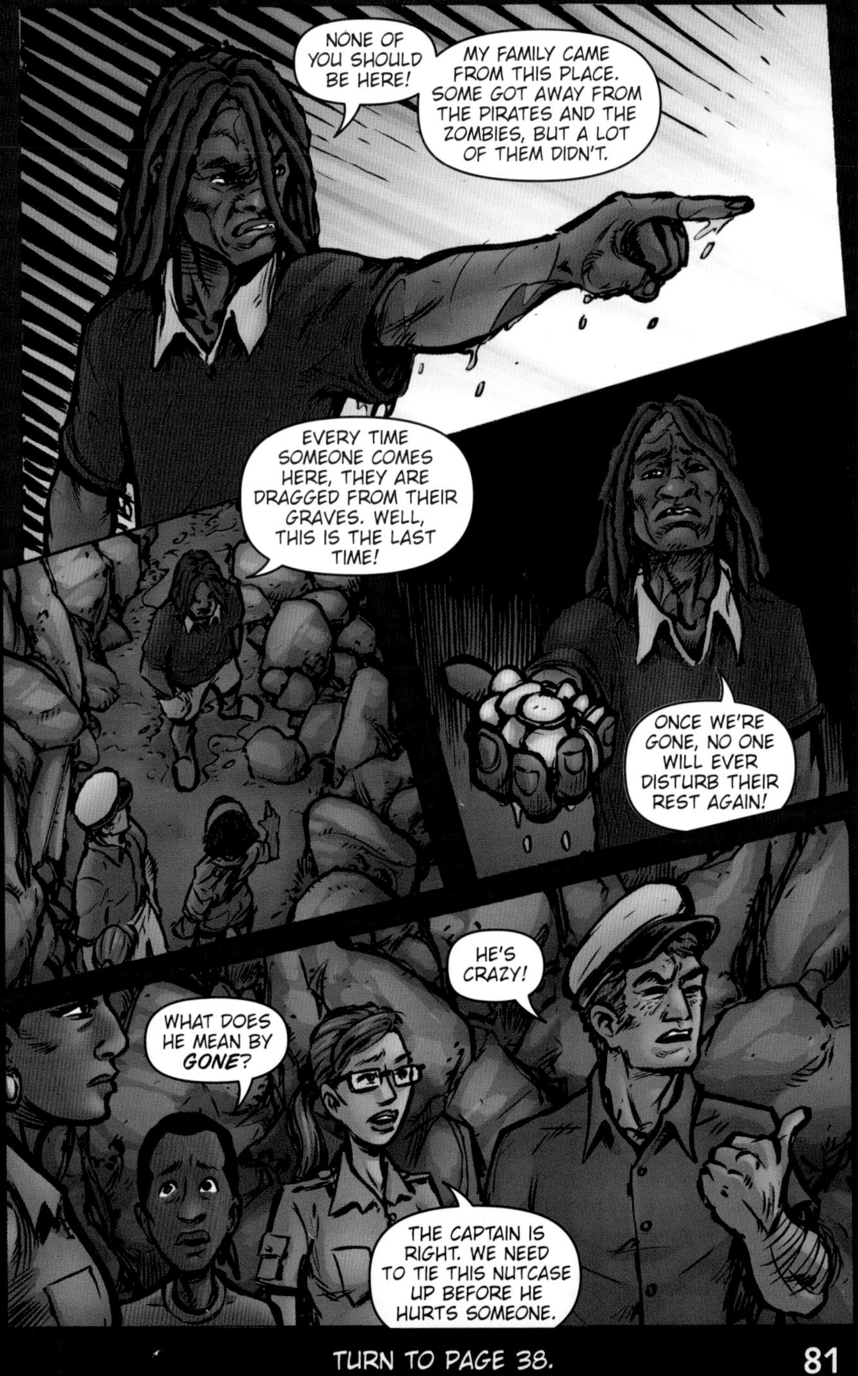
NONE OF YOU SHOULD BE HERE!
MY FAMILY CAME FROM THIS PLACE. SOME GOT AWAY FROM THE PIRATES AND THE ZOMBIES, BUT A LOT OF THEM DIDN'T.
EVERY TIME SOMEONE COMES HERE, THEY ARE DRAGGED FROM THEIR GRAVES. WELL, THIS IS THE LAST TIME!
ONCE WE'RE GONE, NO ONE WILL EVER DISTURB THEIR REST AGAIN!
HE'S CRAZY!
WHAT DOES HE MEAN BY *GONE*?
THE CAPTAIN IS RIGHT. WE NEED TO TIE THIS NUTCASE UP BEFORE HE HURTS SOMEONE.

TURN TO PAGE 38.

After a second, you say, 'Okay! But don't use your torch. He might see.'

The two of you start off towards the beach, darting around trees in the scattered moon-light. In the darkness you and Jimmy trip over unseen roots and fallen branches, but manage to stay on your feet.

Suddenly, you hear something ahead. Grunts, groans and thumps. The sounds of fighting. Then a loud scream echoes through the trees.

'W-was that the captain?' Jimmy asks.

'Maybe the zombies got him,' you reply, trying to make a joke. Somehow, it doesn't sound like one.

'That's stupid,' Jimmy says uncertainly. 'Let's sneak over and see.'

As you creep closer, you see Jimmy pull the pot of salt out of his pocket. Nodding, you do the same.

GO ON TO THE NEXT PAGE.

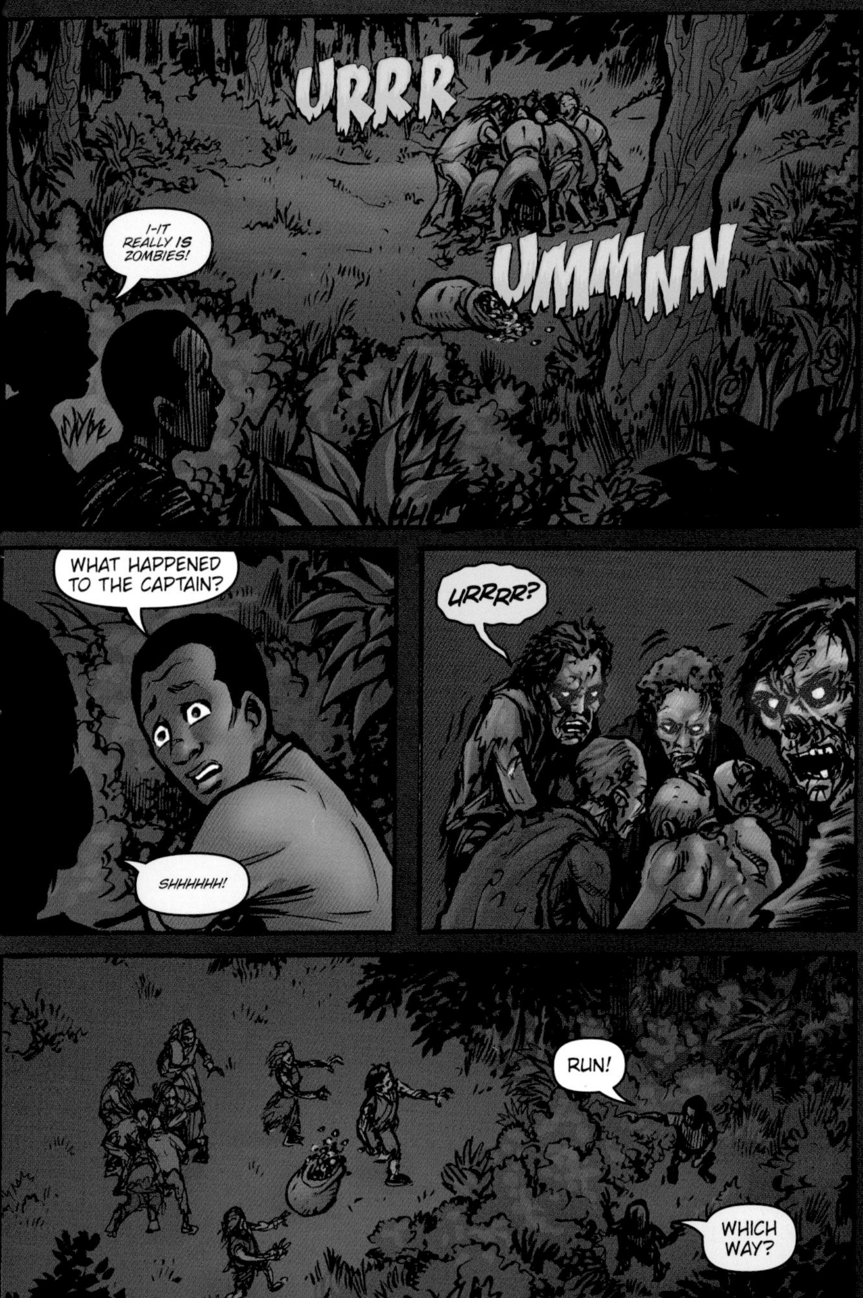
URRR
I-IT REALLY IS ZOMBIES!
UMMNN
WHAT HAPPENED TO THE CAPTAIN?
SHHHHHH!
URRRR?
RUN!
WHICH WAY?

GO ON TO THE NEXT PAGE.

WILL YOU . . .

. . . try to run to the motorboat at the beach?
TURN TO PAGE 65.

. . . try to run back to camp?
TURN TO PAGE 93.

'I think we should go with Dylan,' you tell Dr Chase.

'He's scared you with all those stories, hasn't he?' she says. She seems a bit angry, but she just says, 'Why don't you and Jimmy go down to the lagoon. Tell Dylan I said you can sleep on the *Marlin* tonight. How does that sound?'

You say it sounds okay. You want to tell her everyone should come, but she's not in a mood to listen.

'Come on, Jimmy!' you say. ' I'll race you!'

The two of you run down the path towards the lagoon.

When you get there, you see Dylan in the motorboat, getting the engine ready to go. You tell him what Dr Chase said.

'I wish they had all come,' he says sadly.

'Should we go and get them?' asks Jimmy.

'Too late!' shouts Dylan. 'Look!'

That's when you see the zombies coming out of the shadows beneath the trees!

TURN TO PAGE 98.

'Come on, Dr Chase!' you say. 'If we all carry some, we can have it back here in no time!'

She hesitates a moment then says, 'Alright. It can't hurt to take a look.'

You haven't gone far before Marty whispers, 'Did you hear something? I think there's someone behind us!'

Dr Chase stops and looks around. 'Dylan,' she calls out. 'Is that you?'

The captain shields his eyes with one hand and squints into the shadows beneath the trees. Then he points and says, 'There!'

Now you can all make out a bunch of people walking slowly towards you.

'Who in the world can that be?' says Dr Chase.

You and Jimmy look at each other then back at the figures shambling your way.

'Dylan was right!' you shout.

GO ON TO THE NEXT PAGE.

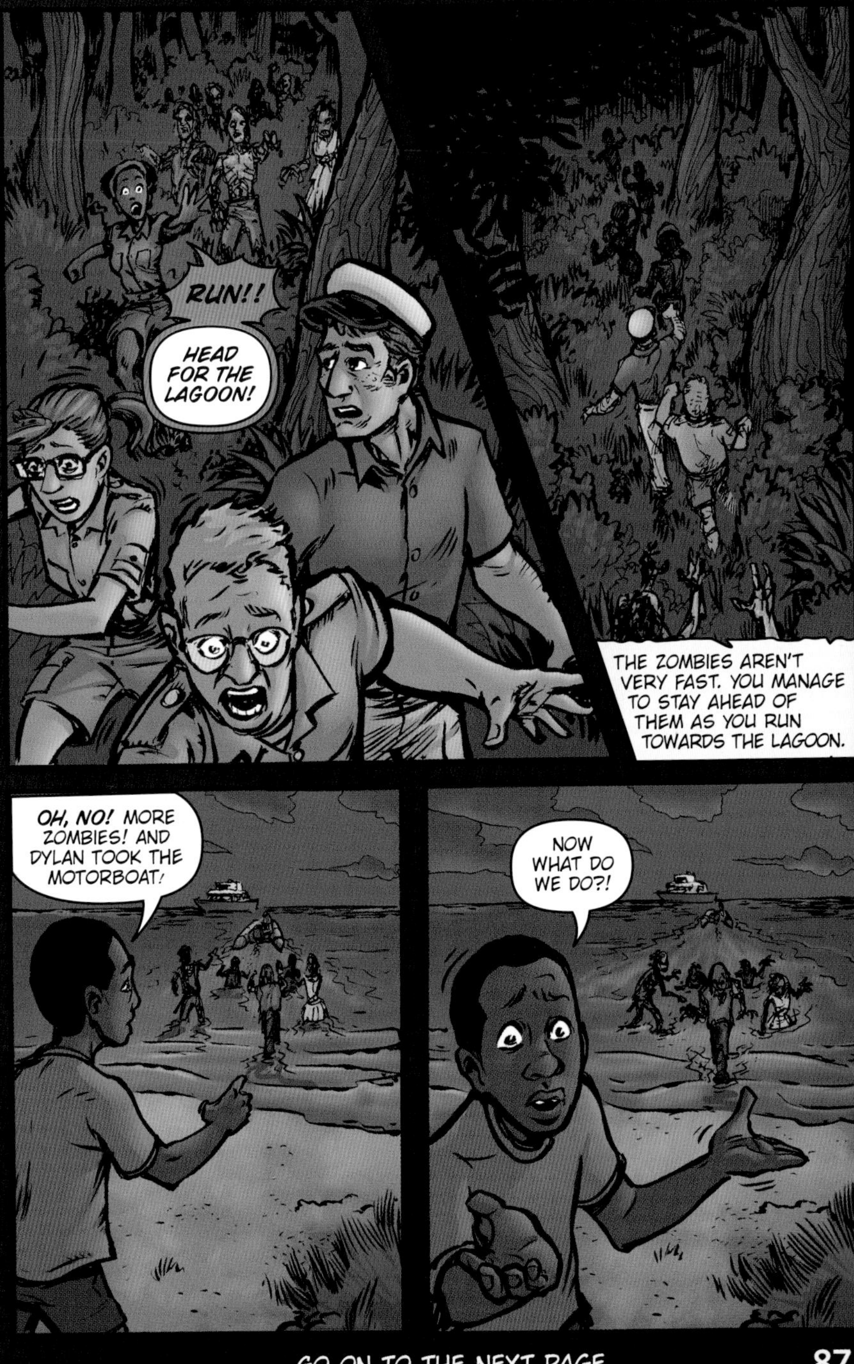
RUN!!
HEAD FOR THE LAGOON!
THE ZOMBIES AREN'T VERY FAST. YOU MANAGE TO STAY AHEAD OF THEM AS YOU RUN TOWARDS THE LAGOON.
OH, NO! MORE ZOMBIES! AND DYLAN TOOK THE MOTORBOAT!
NOW WHAT DO WE DO?!

GO ON TO THE NEXT PAGE.

The others all come crashing out of the trees behind you. Syd is shouting that you need to keep running.

She stops dead, seeing what you've already seen. 'How could he leave us,' she whispers.

Dr Chase has followed her onto the beach. She looks at the zombies in front of you and glances back as the captain and Marty arrive.

'He had no choice,' she says. 'They would have got him too.'

'Now what?' gasps Marty.

'Maybe we can swim!' says Dr Chase. 'Spread out. Try and get around them!'

You all do as she says, running in different directions, trying to dodge the clawlike hands that reach for you.

Ducking away from the sweep of a zombie pirate's sword, you reach the water!

As you dive in, you hear Marty squeal with fear behind you. You keep swimming.

An icy hand grabs your ankle from below. It drags you down, under the water.

THE END

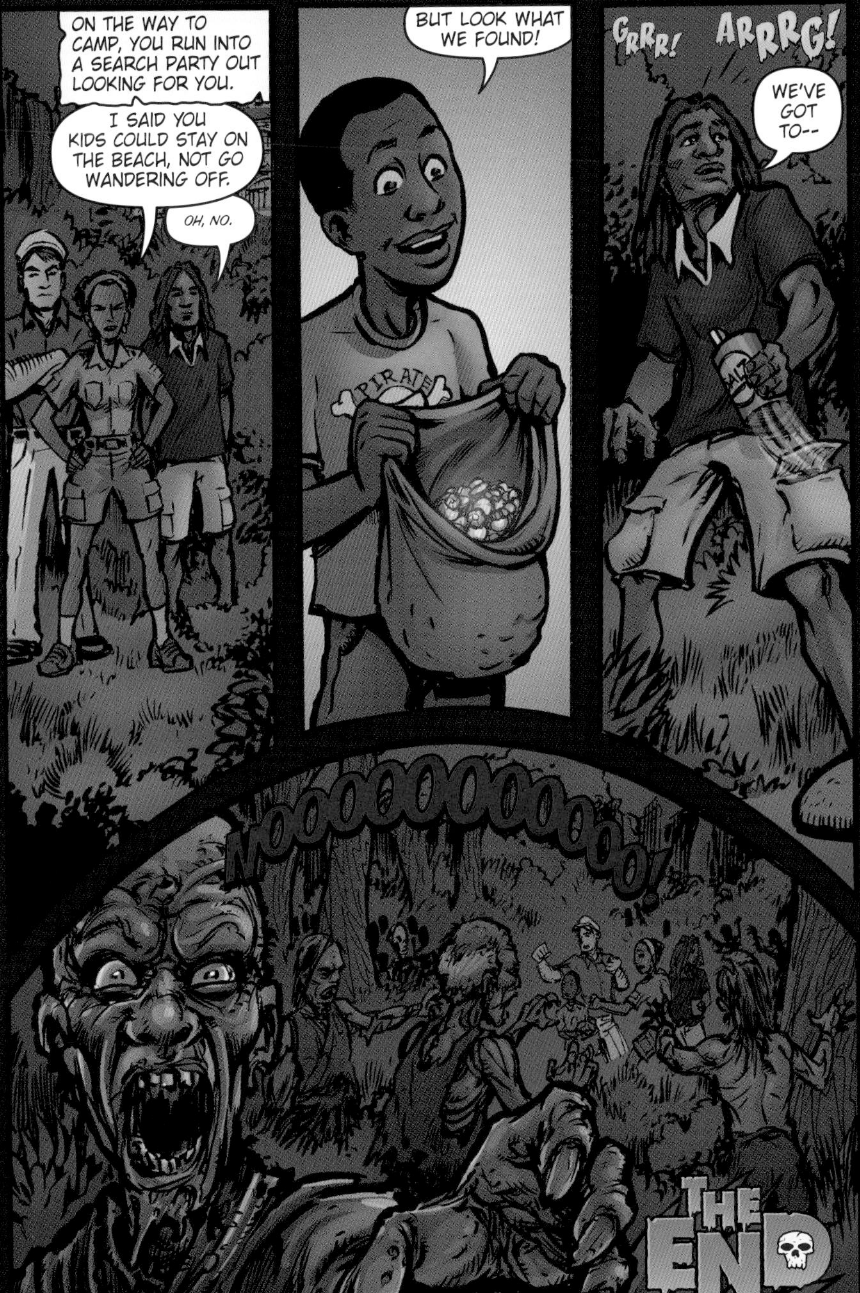
ON THE WAY TO CAMP, YOU RUN INTO A SEARCH PARTY OUT LOOKING FOR YOU.
I SAID YOU KIDS COULD STAY ON THE BEACH, NOT GO WANDERING OFF.
OH, NO.
BUT LOOK WHAT WE FOUND!
GRRR!
ARRRG!
WE'VE GOT TO--
NOOOOOOOOOOOOO!
THE END

You wait a couple of minutes then sneak through the waterfall and into a cave. You're soaked and shivering, but you barely notice. You're in a pirate treasure cave!

Both you and Jimmy keep your torches shielded with your hands so the captain doesn't see. Up ahead, you see a tunnel.

Motioning for Jimmy to keep quiet, you sneak into it. After a while, it opens up into a big cavern. There's a narrow ledge that leads to the far side. You think you see some light from up ahead.

Very carefully, you make your way across.

You wait for Jimmy in front of the tunnel on the other side.

'Where do you think he is?' Jimmy whispers.

'HERE!' shouts the captain, leaping out of the tunnel and switching on his light.

Startled, you jump back, bumping into Jimmy.

You both tumble over the ledge, falling and falling into the darkness below.

THE END

You and Jimmy take the goblets you picked out and sprint through the woods, leaving your backpacks behind. In a few minutes, you find the old plantation house where the others have set up camp.

Jimmy runs up to his aunt, holding out his goblet proudly. 'We found the pirate treasure!' he says. 'In a cave! Behind a waterfall!'

Dylan grabs you by the shoulders and says, 'Why did you take it out of the cave? I told you about the curse!'

Syd, one of Dr Chase's assistants, laughs. 'Don't be silly!' she says. 'Pirate treasure! This is a major historical find.'

Her brother Marty, Dr Chase's other assistant, gulps. 'Curse?' he asks.

'We need to get off this island right now!' says Dylan. 'It may already be too late!'

Syd rolls her eyes. 'We should take a look right away, Dr Chase.'

'I'll help,' says the captain. 'It's bound to be heavy.'

GO ON TO THE NEXT PAGE.

WILL YOU . . .

. . . try to get off the island like Dylan says?
TURN TO PAGE 69.

. . . show them where the treasure is?
TURN TO PAGE 102.

With the zombies right behind, you and Jimmy run as fast as you can towards the camp. A couple of times you throw some salt over your shoulder at them. You're not sure if it works, but you think you hear some of them falling over.

You burst into camp, shouting loudly for everyone to wake up! A second later, people start to come out of the tents.

No! Not people! *'Zombies!'*

The two of you skid to a stop as the zombies lurch towards you.

Together, you yell, 'The motorboat!'

You both turn to run the other way. You slam into something heavy and fall to the ground. You look up into the wide, white eyes of a zombie. Drool hangs from the corners of a mouth full of twisted, yellow teeth. Withered hands hold a rusty cutlass raised high.

Then the sword slices down on you.

THE END

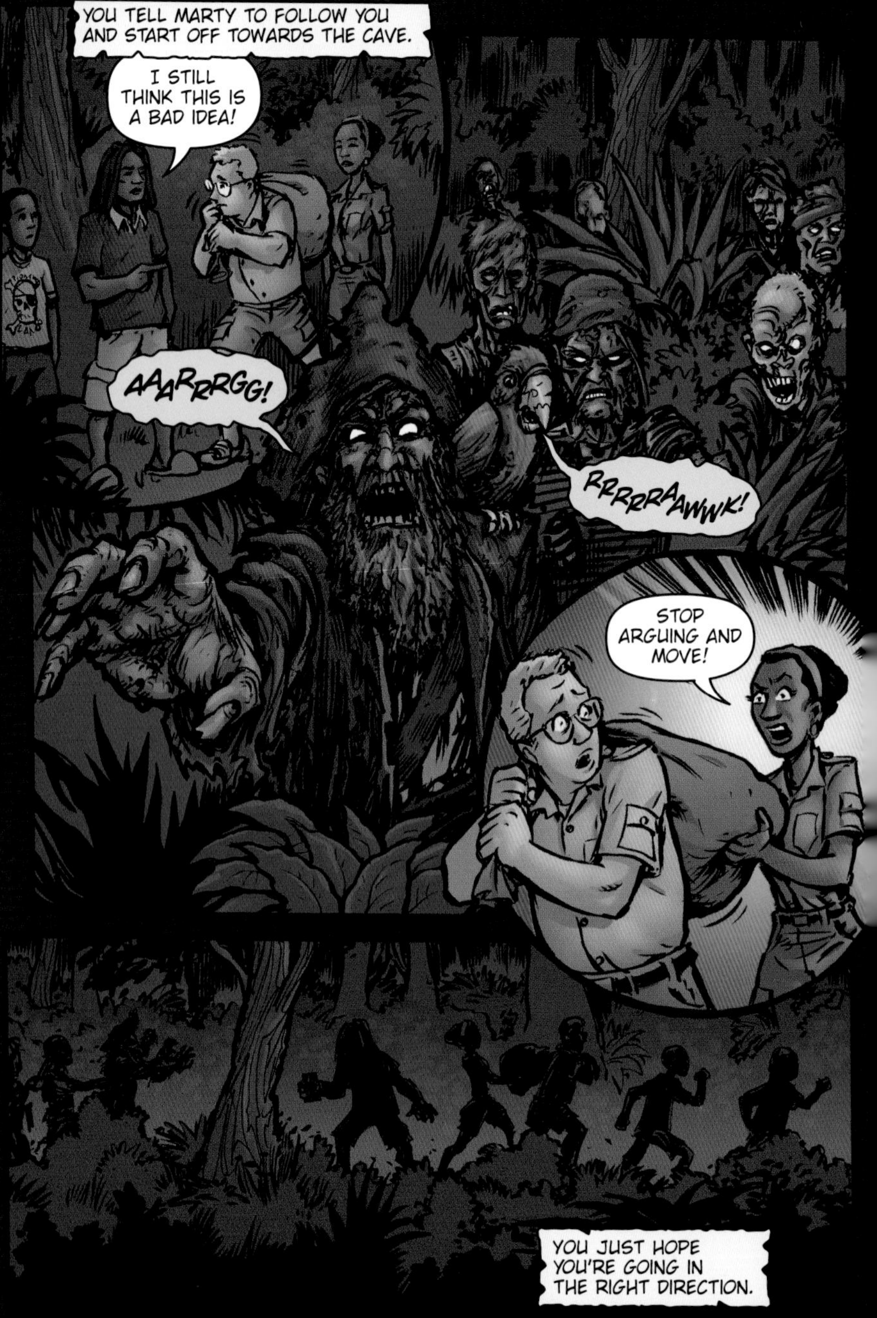
YOU TELL MARTY TO FOLLOW YOU AND START OFF TOWARDS THE CAVE.
I STILL THINK THIS IS A BAD IDEA!
AAARRRGG!
RRRRRAAWWK!
STOP ARGUING AND MOVE!
YOU JUST HOPE YOU'RE GOING IN THE RIGHT DIRECTION.

GO ON TO THE NEXT PAGE.

You manage to stay ahead of the zombies, but you can hear them shuffling. It seems like forever, but you finally hear the sound of splashing water.

Following it, you come out of the trees into the clearing by the waterfall.

Gasping for air, Marty trips and falls to the ground.

Dr Chase grabs at the bag and yells for Dylan to help her.

The two of them haul the bag towards the waterfall as the zombies lurch into the clearing. With a great effort, Dr Chase and Dylan hurl the bag through the plunging water and into the cave beyond.

The zombies take one more step. Two steps. You clutch at a handful of salt, ready to throw it.

Then the zombies turn and walk away!

'I don't believe it,' Dylan gasps. 'They're returning to their graves!'

'Way to go, Marty!' you cheer.

THE END

'What about the curse, Dr Chase?' you ask. 'Maybe we should leave it be.'

She smiles. 'I don't believe in curses, but if it will make you feel better, we'll leave it for now and come back tomorrow.'

As you head back to camp, the captain grumbles about walking all that way for nothing.

When you enter the clearing around the plantation house, you're surprised to see a crowd of people filling the space.

'Who are you?' Dr Chase calls out angrily. 'What are you doing here?'

They turn slowly, the moonlight shining on their pale dead faces and dirty, tattered clothes.

'Zombies!' gasps the captain.

'But we didn't take anything,' you say.

Jimmy lets out a moan. As the zombies come shuffling towards you, he pulls a handful of gold coins from a pocket.

'I didn't think there would be any harm,' he whispers.

THE END

WILL YOU . . .

. . . follow the shadowy figure?
TURN TO PAGE 35.

. . . let Dr Chase know about it?
TURN TO PAGE 39.

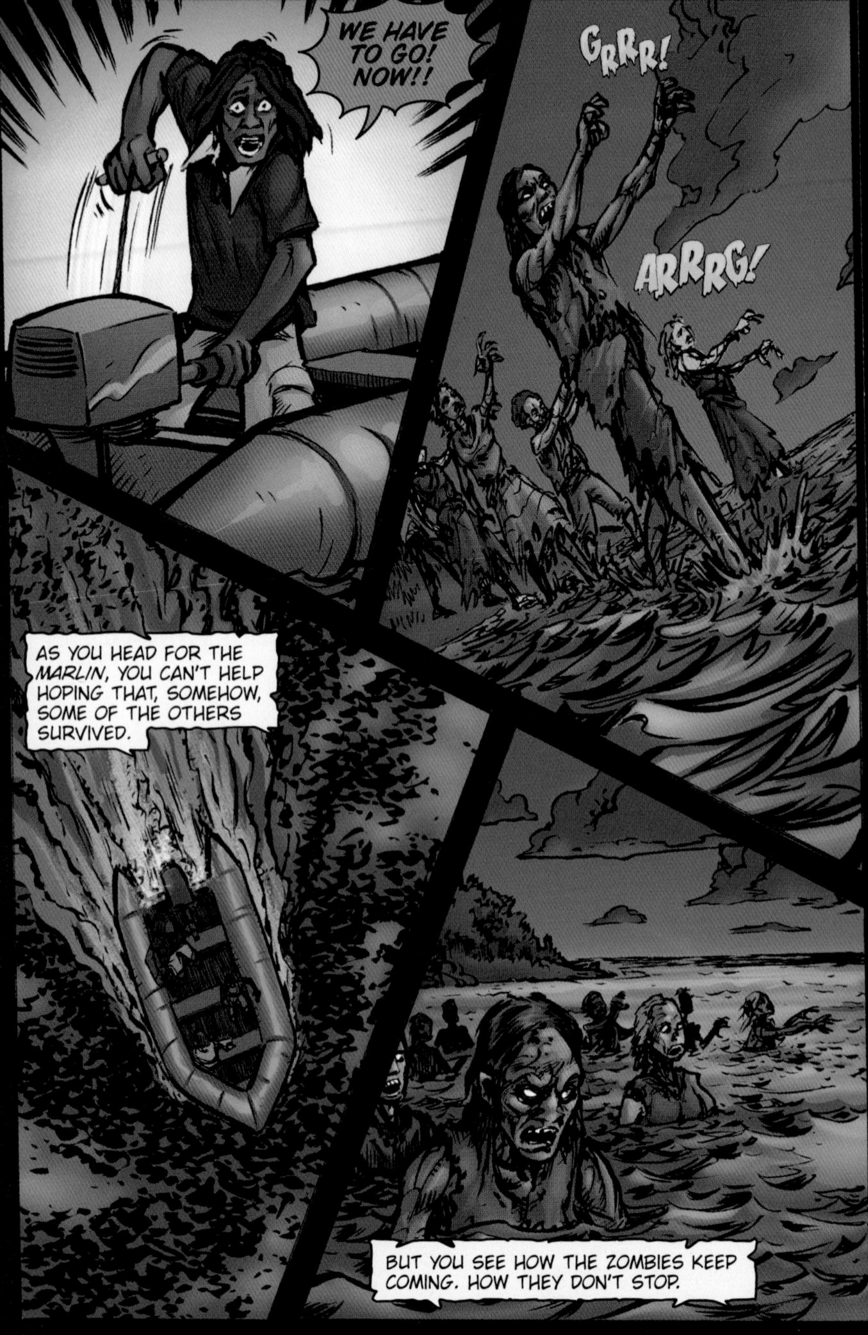
WE HAVE TO GO! NOW!!
GRRR!
ARRRG!
AS YOU HEAD FOR THE *MARLIN*, YOU CAN'T HELP HOPING THAT, SOMEHOW, SOME OF THE OTHERS SURVIVED.
BUT YOU SEE HOW THE ZOMBIES KEEP COMING. HOW THEY DON'T STOP.

GO ON TO THE NEXT PAGE.

As Dylan ties the smaller boat up to the *Marlin*, you see the heads of the zombies disappear into the water. 'I think they're still coming,' you say. 'Under the water.'

Dylan helps you and Jimmy up the ladder. 'It'll be okay,' he says. 'Once we're in open seas, we'll be fine.'

'How do you know?' you ask.

'I was right about the other stuff, wasn't I?' he says.

You can't argue with that.

Dylan rushes to the wheel-house. He throws the switch to raise the anchor and starts the engine.

You and Jimmy look back at the island.

'Maybe the others . . . ' he starts. Then his voice fades.

'Maybe,' you say.

But as the *Marlin* heads out to sea, you know, deep down, that the three of you were the only ones to escape from Zombie Island.

THE END

'Let's just go back,' you say.

'Okay,' Jimmy says. 'I'm tired from all that stuff we did this morning.'

When you don't reach the camp after several minutes, you realize you're both more tired than you thought. Somehow you got off track!

'Which way?' Jimmy asks, yawning.

'That way,' you say, pointing.

'You sure?' he asks.

You shrug.

He starts to argue, but you hear someone coming towards you through the trees.

You both shine your torches into the darkness, trying to see who it is.

'Dylan?' you whisper. 'Is that you?'

Just then, your beam reveals someone in the shadows. A woman in a torn and dirty dress. She steps towards you, moaning. Then you see there are others behind her.

'Zombies! They're real!' Jimmy screams.

You turn to run, but they are all around. Their clutching hands reach out.

You wish your parents had never let you come . . .

THE END

100

WILL YOU . . .

... decide it's not worth the bother?
TURN TO PAGE ??.

... volunteer to get Dylan?
TURN TO PAGE 37.

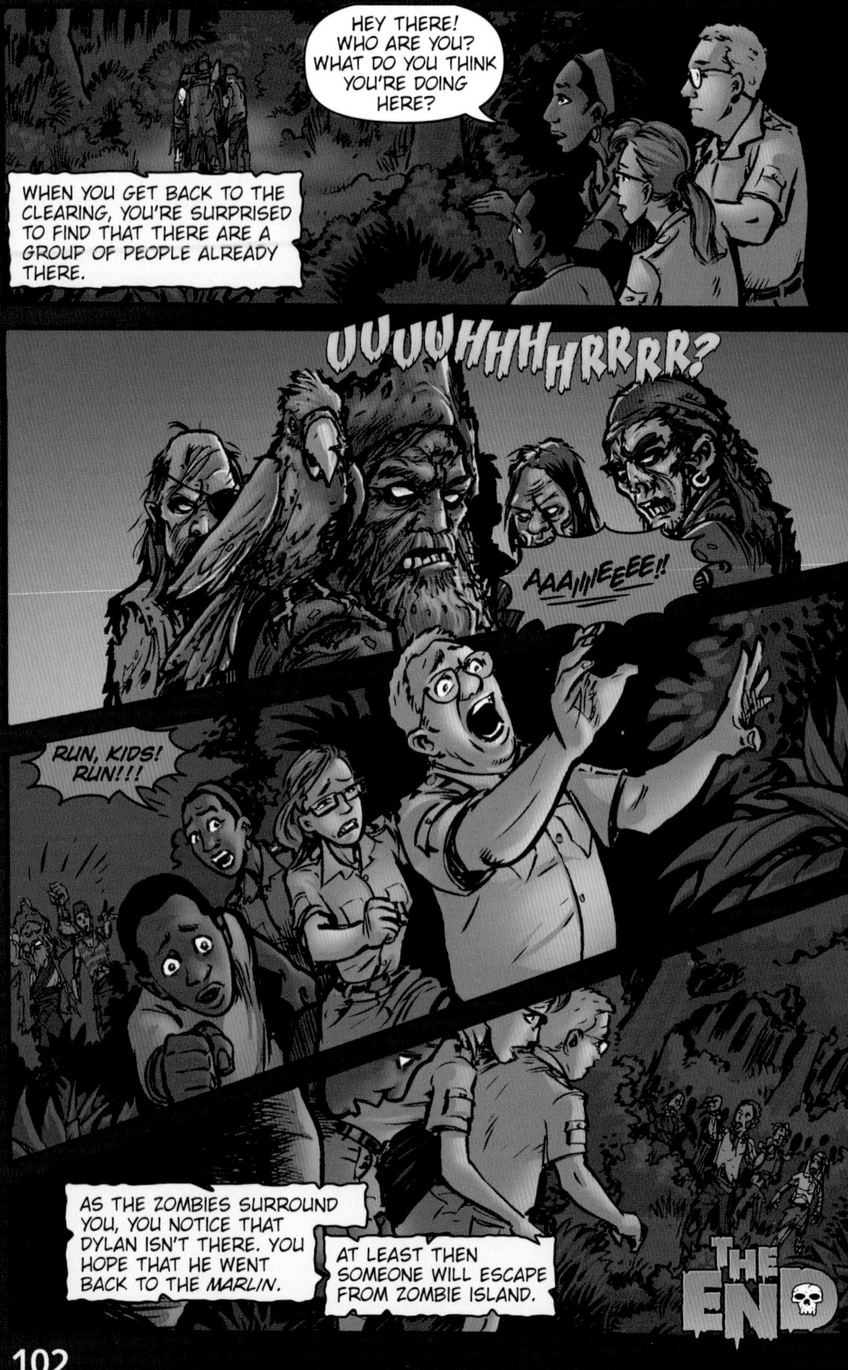
HEY THERE! WHO ARE YOU? WHAT DO YOU THINK YOU'RE DOING HERE?
WHEN YOU GET BACK TO THE CLEARING, YOU'RE SURPRISED TO FIND THAT THERE ARE A GROUP OF PEOPLE ALREADY THERE.
UUUUHHHHRRRRR?
AAAIIIIEEEE!!
RUN, KIDS! RUN!!!
AS THE ZOMBIES SURROUND YOU, YOU NOTICE THAT DYLAN ISN'T THERE. YOU HOPE THAT HE WENT BACK TO THE *MARLIN*.
AT LEAST THEN SOMEONE WILL ESCAPE FROM ZOMBIE ISLAND.
THE END

You and Jimmy decide to bury the treasure under the trees. You pick one with a twisted trunk that you're sure you'll be able to find again.

After you drag the backpacks over, Jimmy asks, 'What are we going to use for shovels?'

You think for a little bit. 'Fallen branches?' Jimmy nods and starts looking around for some.

You find a couple of good ones and start to dig.

After a few minutes, you hear someone coming through the trees.

'Great,' you say to Jimmy. 'Now what do we do?'

'I don't know,' says Jimmy. 'Maybe . . .'

A large group of people shuffle out of the shadows. Their clothes are old and dirty. As they come, you hear them moaning and groaning. Their hands are stretched out, twisted like claws.

'They look like . . .' Jimmy says.

'Zombies!' you scream together.

You try to run, but they're all around you . . .

THE END

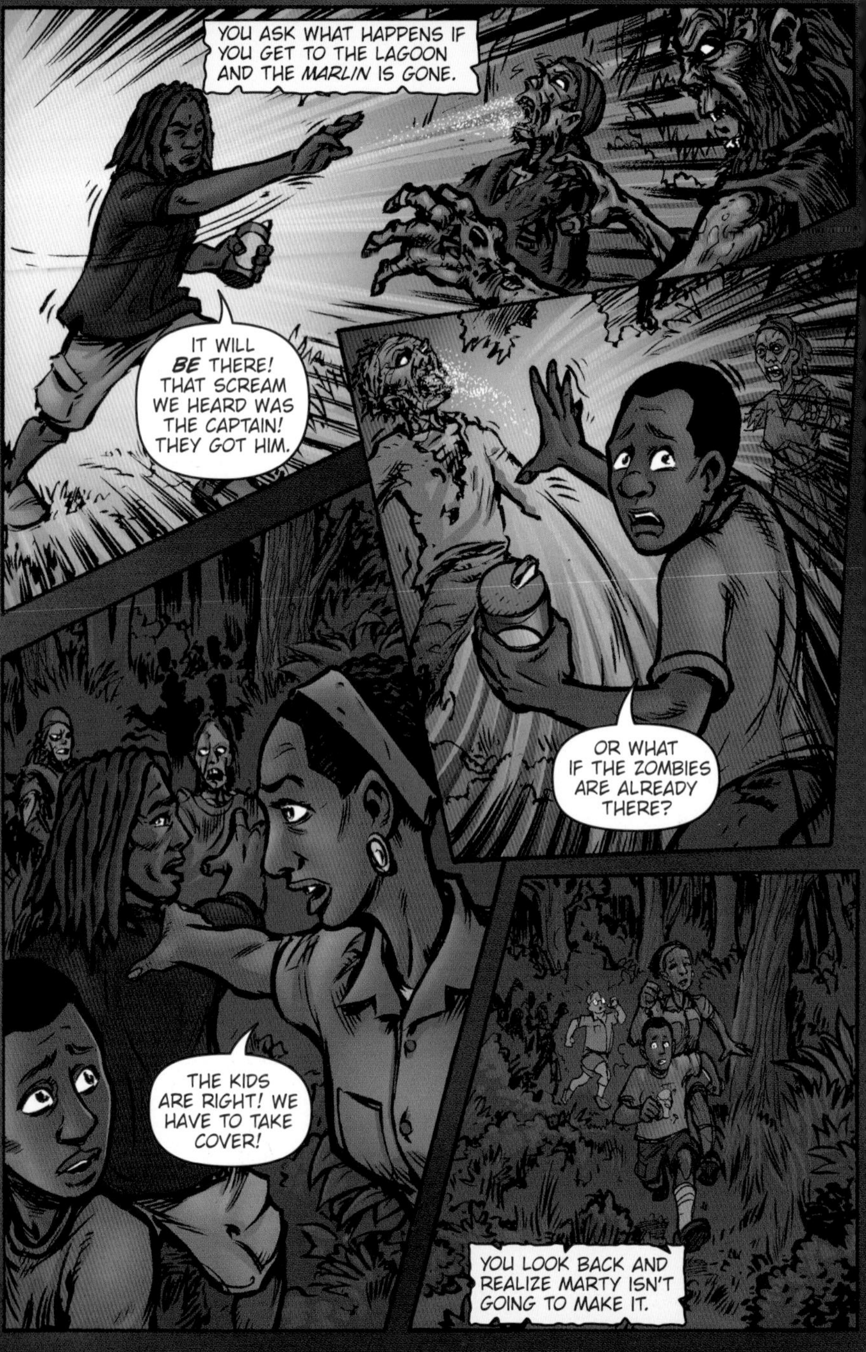
YOU ASK WHAT HAPPENS IF YOU GET TO THE LAGOON AND THE *MARLIN* IS GONE.
IT WILL ***BE*** THERE! THAT SCREAM WE HEARD WAS THE CAPTAIN! THEY GOT HIM.
OR WHAT IF THE ZOMBIES ARE ALREADY THERE?
THE KIDS ARE RIGHT! WE HAVE TO TAKE COVER!
YOU LOOK BACK AND REALIZE MARTY ISN'T GOING TO MAKE IT.

GO ON TO THE NEXT PAGE.

You hear Marty cry out as you run up the porch steps. What's left of the doors almost crumbles as you push through.

Inside is a big room, with a wide staircase leading to the second floor. Right in front of you is a big hole, where something heavy crashed through the floor. You shout back, 'Which way?'

Dr Chase yells that you should go upstairs. 'Higher ground!' she says.

Going around the hole, you start up the stairs. You call back, 'Come on! Come on!'

As the others hurry into the house, you run up the stairs. Then you hear a loud cracking sound!

The stairway is rotten! The stairs break underneath your feet!

You lose your grip on your torch.

As you plunge into darkness, you can hear the *thump-thump-thump* of the torch rolling down the stairs.

After that, you hear nothing at all . . .

THE END

You say, 'What if we get it to the cave and it doesn't work? What do we do then?'

Jimmy agrees. So does Dr Chase.

Dylan gestures towards the lagoon. 'C'mon! They're coming!'

All of you start that way, except for Marty. He starts to wrestle with the bag. 'Go on, then,' he says. 'Just tell me which way to the cave. Just in case.'

You turn back to argue, to convince Marty he has to come with you, when the zombies stagger out of the shadows behind him.

'Marty!' you shout. 'Look out!'

It's too late though. The zombies grab him, pulling him down. You turn to run with the rest of the group as Marty starts to scream.

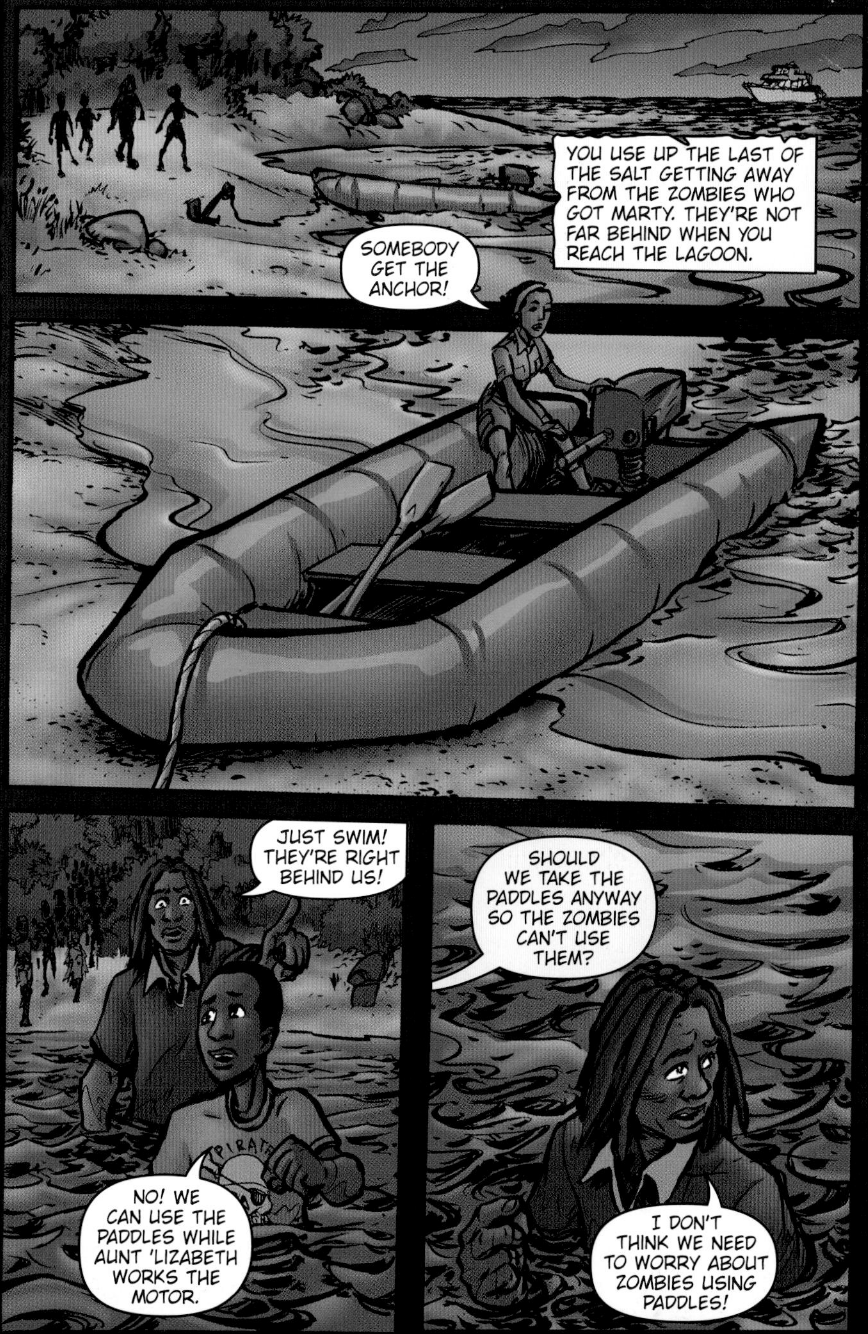
YOU USE UP THE LAST OF THE SALT GETTING AWAY FROM THE ZOMBIES WHO GOT MARTY. THEY'RE NOT FAR BEHIND WHEN YOU REACH THE LAGOON.
SOMEBODY GET THE ANCHOR!
JUST SWIM! THEY'RE RIGHT BEHIND US!
NO! WE CAN USE THE PADDLES WHILE AUNT 'LIZABETH WORKS THE MOTOR.
SHOULD WE TAKE THE PADDLES ANYWAY SO THE ZOMBIES CAN'T USE THEM?
I DON'T THINK WE NEED TO WORRY ABOUT ZOMBIES USING PADDLES!

GO ON TO THE NEXT PAGE.

WILL YOU . . .

... tell Dr Chase to start the engine?
TURN TO PAGE 21.

... swim and take the paddles with you?
TURN TO PAGE 62.

... use the paddles while
she tries to start the engine?
TURN TO PAGE 42.

... just swim for it?
TURN TO PAGE 110.

Time drags as you watch the waterfall. Finally, the captain splashes back out.

He's carrying a big canvas bag. When he sets it down to rest, treasure spills out.

Jimmy gasps. You clamp your hand over his mouth, but it's too late.

'Come on out,' says the captain, shining his torch your way. He's got a pistol in his other hand!

Reluctantly, the two of you do what he says.

He ties you both up with your own shoelaces, laughing the whole time.

'This treasure is mine, you know! That pirate Dylan told you about was my great-great grandpa! My family always knew he hid his treasure in some cave behind a waterfall. We just didn't know which island it was on. When Dylan told me that zombie story, I couldn't believe my luck!'

Just then, you see something in the trees behind him. Zombies!

The captain's luck has run out.

Yours too . . .

THE END

'Okay, forget the oars!' you yell. 'Let's just swim!'

Everyone dives into the water and heads for the *Marlin*.

As you reach it, you look back. The zombies have climbed into the motorboat, and they're paddling your way!

Dylan scrambles up the ladder. Dr Chase helps Jimmy up next, but his hands, trembling with fear, lose their grip. He falls back into the water onto his aunt.

First Dylan gets the motor started. Then he comes back to help the rest of you onboard. Finally, you collapse exhausted on deck.

Dylan starts for the wheelhouse, but slips on the wet deck. Staggering to his feet, he moves carefully to take the wheel.

You all give a ragged cheer, just as something thumps the hull. Turning back, you watch in horror as zombies haul themselves over the rail . . .

THE END